OUT ON
A LIMB
Handling Life's Challenges

∽

by

ABEL DAVIS

". . .and she again bore his brother Abel. And Abel was a keeper of the sheep. . .And Abel, he also brought of the firstlings of his flock and of the fat thereof. And the Lord had respect unto Abel and to his offering."
—Genesis 4:2 & 4

Granite Publishing and Distribution
Orem, Utah

Published and Distributed by:

PUBLISHING & DISTRIBUTION L.L.C.

Granite Publishing and Distribution, L.L.C.
270 S. Mountainlands Dr.
Orem, UT 84058
(801) 229-9023

FIRST EDITION
ISBN: 1-890558-29-X

Printed in the United States of America

For Speaking engagements please write:
P.O. Box 2271
Sandy, UT 84091
Or call toll free 1-877-IAM-ABEL

Typesetting done by Myrna Maughan Varga, The Office Connection – Provo, Utah

For Wendy

There are those who have met disaster, which almost seems defeat, who have become somewhat soured in their natures. But if they stop to think, even the adversity which has come to them may prove a means of spiritual uplift.

Adversity, itself, may lead toward enlightenment; and privation may prove a source of strength, if we can but keep a sweetness of mind and spirit.

—David O. McKay

Contents

Acknowledgments

$\mathcal{T}$he fruition of this book was made possible by family, friends and acquaintances. I wish to thank and acknowledge the following:

My Mom and Dad, for their incredible moral support and for teaching me to believe in myself.

Wendy, my precious love, who tenderly encouraged me to pursue my dream. For the numerous hours of reading, proofing and editing the first draft. I love you!

Mark, Glen, Kent, Lisa, Brook, Janna and Rob, faithful brothers and sisters whom I regard as shining examples of living principled lives.

Alice Edvalson, a dear friend, for sharing *The Spellbinder's Gift* which, ultimately, inspired me to write this book.

Darol Wagstaff, a mentor, for the numerous years of coaching and influencing me to become a seasoned professional speaker and for his complimentary forward.

Sandra Watts, beloved mother-in-law, for her expertise in

syntax, grammar, punctuation and proper English corrections.

Brad Hill, a friend, for the positive feedback and for the clever "hook" written on the back cover.

Clyde E. Weeks, Jr., an author, for the numerous hours of editing and bringing this book to its high state of excellence.

Foreword

---

*I*n 1990, I received a telephone call from Abel Davis. He asked me, "What do I need to do to become a professional speaker?" I get several calls like this every week, so I usually ask the aspiring speaker if they have identified a message that is unique to them. It didn't take me long to realize that Abel's story was, at the very least, "unique."

Abel was born and reared in a mountain village in the Bolivian Andes. When he was four-years-old, he herded one hundred sheep with the help of his pony. His father worked at a sugar cane factory. One day, he went to the outside factory to visit his father. That day, Abel had a devastating accident that changed the course of his life: he became, simultaneously, an orphan and an amputee.

The day I met Abel, I felt fortunate. Abel's influence has encouraged thousands of people to believe that they are able, too—including me. His story can be interpreted as tragic, but Abel has never seen it that way.

As you read this book, Abel's humor and wit will comfort

you when you are tempted to cry; his wisdom and life experience will commit you to never give up; and when you are at a loss for direction, his faith and belief in the capability of the human spirit will inspire you to achieve greatness, so that your contribution to society will make the world a stronger and better place.

After all, since a very young age, Abel has understood the correlation between a shepherd and his sheep. Abel has a strong devotion to and appreciation for the "Master Shepherd." He is committed to "the one." Probably, because throughout his life, the "ninety and nine" have been left by other shepherds who have "gone into the mountains" after him. His philosophy is that the world can be motivated, one person at a time.

Since our first conversation, Abel has spoken across North America to people from all walks of life: students and student leaders, teachers, parents, corporate employees and executives. He is especially dedicated to kids in children's hospitals, and has spent hundreds of hours speaking to the youth in juvenile detention centers.

Now, you are the fortuitous one. You have in your hands a very powerful tool. Abel will be a friend, and a mentor to you, as you read his book. If you want to get to know him better, write him a letter: he will write you back. Or if you want to talk with him, give him a phone call. But for now, curl up in your favorite chair for a quiet evening of reading—it won't take you long to realize that *you are able*, too.

Darol Wagstaff, President
Champions for Life Speakers Bureau
Salt Lake City, Utah

Preface

---

*W*e have all asked ourselves questions similar to these: Where did I come from? Did I evolve from a monkey which lived millions of years ago, or was I created by God? What am I doing here? What is my ultimate purpose of mortal life? Where do I go from here? What is to become of me after I pass away? Is there another life, or is this it?

Scientists, theologians, scholars and others have attempted to answer these incomprehensible questions with their theories, trying to convince us their ideology is right. However, it seems the more they theorize, the more complicated their answers become.

I like to think that life does not have to be *that* complex, understanding that we have a limited knowledge of our past and future. Rather, concentrating on the present is what we need to do, because that is where we exist.

> *Look to this day, for it is the very life of life. In its brief course lie all of the verities and*

> *realities of your existence—the glory of action, the bliss of growth, the splendor of beauty. For yesterday is but a dream and tomorrow only a vision; but today well lived makes every yesterday a dream of happiness and every tomorrow a vision of hope. Look well, therefore, to this day.*
>
> —From The Sanskrit

Knowing our history may help us cope with the present, but I believe we learn more about ourselves from the experiences we encounter, the challenges we face. If we constructively master the lessons derived from the various events throughout our lives, we will become better individuals, physically, mentally and emotionally, thus giving us a launching pad to face the future.

My religious background and personal beliefs give me assurance of my purpose in life. But more importantly, these fundamental convictions supply me with principles, morals and values which I choose to live by, which in essence give me strength, courage, and power to accept the currents of life's challenges—like a paper boat on a stream.

As a young child, do you remember making one of these paper boats and, excitedly, dropping it into the water of the nearby ditch and following it along the waters' edge, as the current carried it through a maze of drifts, turns and bends? Metaphorically, we are all like paper boats, floating down stream. Sometimes, the current carries us through choppy waters, giving us a sinking feeling, making it difficult to stay afloat.

Other times, the tides will cascade us to the edges of awaiting waterfalls, giving us cause to fear drowning, and alerting us to the importance of life jackets in the event we do go overboard. Yet, the current most often takes us to calm and tranquil waters where we bask in the warmth of the sun's rays and marvel at the awesomeness of this grand universe.

No doubt, life is filled with turns, bends, rapids, waterfalls and calm, soothing waters, and why shouldn't it be? An amalgamation of good and bad. And just as the paper boat was helped along by a young, caring hand, we, too, are given helping hands to help, motivate, uplift, encourage, love, strengthen and discipline us, as we traverse through the different currents of life. The story I am about to tell you is about just that—helping hands.

Before I continue, I want to suggest the tremendous effort it took for me to write this book. For several years now, I have wanted to write about my life. Many people have heard my story and have encouraged me to write a book. Every time I determined to proceed with the project, I would think of excuses to convince myself that I should not proceed with such a monumental project.

It wasn't until I read Og Mandino's *The Spellbinder's Gift,* a book given to me by a dear friend, that I was motivated, powerfully enough, to seek the realization of my dream.

While reading *The Spellbinder's Gift,* I was moved by the compassion exhibited by one of the main characters, Patrick Donne. He was a simple man who had devoted his efforts to enhancing the lives of many people with his unpretentious, yet profound, wisdom. It was the simple act of love, Christ-like love, eloquently demonstrated by Patrick Donne, which compelled me to listen to my inward thoughts and, like Pat, to commit my endeavors to serve others through sharing my story.

It is my hope and prayer, as one reads my story, that they may discover their own uniqueness and realize that they are, individually, important. And no matter what the consequences, trials and hardships we suffer, we all have the ability to become someone remarkable. We have been granted life in this wonderful world to reap the bounteous blessings, stored for those who seek to find them. I am one of those recipients of life's many rewards.

In 1966 Lyndon B. Johnson was serving his third year as President of the United States. The Vietnam War was escalating to greater proportions. Peace and love were the main themes of the "hippie" generation. The Apollo 16 moon mission was in its preliminary stages. Color television was then making waves in American homes, and, somewhere in a small village high in the Bolivian Andes, I, Abel Padilla Pedraza, was born.

My beloved birth country is a landlocked republic in central South America. Bolivia is bordered on the north and east by Brazil, on the southeast by Paraguay, on the south by Argentina, and on the southwest and west by Chile and Peru. Bolivia is a country that has been richly blessed with natural resources. However, high costs of production, inadequate internal transport, lack of investment, and its being a landlocked nation have limited the country's development.

Bolivia remains, today, one of the poorest countries in South America and the entire world.

CHAPTER 1

Humble Beginnings

I was born in the southern section of Bolivia in the small village of Mojocoya in the province of Chuquisaca. My memory is unclear and my recollection uncertain about all the particulars of my birth and my surroundings. However, I have been able to extract some information to explain the particulars of my birth, family and living conditions. Even though I do not have complete details of my beginnings, this does not prevent me from sharing what I do recall of a pivotal period in my life.

In Bolivia it is not uncommon for the wealthy to live in the cities and the poor to live in the mountains. So it was with my family. Home was in the hills of Mojocoya overlooking the underdeveloped village. My father built our simple home with adobe blocks (a mixture of mud and straw). The house was most likely the size of a modest American living room. The roof that covered our house was fabricated of rusted tin scraps. The floor was dirt, hardened after our constant traffic. We did not have indoor plumbing or running water of any kind.

Electricity would have been a luxury. That, of course, meant that we did not have such luxuries as televisions, stereos, refrigerators, ranges, microwaves, etc. We did not even know that such things existed. Nonetheless, our home satisfied the needs of our modest desires.

Some of the earlier recollections of my youth (under the age of four) were doing many chores around our home. Father was a farmer. I can remember him working from the time the roosters crowed in the brisk mornings, until after the sun set over the Andes and the hens crouched to nest. He cultivated the land with ox-drawn plows and, on occasion, hunted over the mountain to find food for our family.

One particular evening, he returned from one of those excursions with a black Puma cat, draped over his shoulders. I don't remember eating this fresh catch, but I am certain, if I had, it would have tasted like chicken, as the saying goes.

Dressed in the traditional indigenous attire, a full umbrella skirt dragging to the floor, a colorful blanket strapped around her neck and the familiar derby hat, mother, by tradition, was the homemaker. The wrinkles on her brown face and the streaks of gray hair were her emblems of hardship. Her responsibilities were many: cooking, cleaning, washing, and watching over the welfare of her children. I cannot ever recall her complaining of the manner in which she had to go about doing her duties.

Cooking, I am sure, was no easy task. Meals were prepared just outside of our door in a pot over charcoals. Day in and day out, bending over to stir the food must have been strenuous to her fragile body. Unwavering, she fulfilled her obligations to her children, husband, and home.

My parents instilled in me the value of work at an early age. The labors of my parents never brought riches or wealth to our lives. It did not bring prestige or accolades from others. They taught me something deeper, something more profound. Their example of hard work brought to the surface the embodiment of the proverbial Old Testament scripture — By the sweat of thy face thou shalt labor all the days of thy life.

No matter what their circumstances, no matter what their situations, no matter their challenges, they never lost sight of their responsibilities as parents. Their primary obligation was our needs. Whether it was my father with a wearied body working the ox-drawn plows, or my mother with worn hands, mending tattered clothes, both fulfilled their callings of parenting with integrity and dignity.

So it was, without surprise, that the value of work was taught to us (perhaps out of necessity) by my parents, almost in our infancy. However, chores done by American children, I never had to do in my native country. For example, I never had to vacuum. It would have been difficult to vacuum an uncarpeted floor. I didn't have to mop. Even if I had tried I would have only created mud on the dirt floor. I didn't wash dishes, because mother or my sisters usually had that responsibility, thank goodness. I never made my bed because I didn't have one—it wasn't uncommon for the whole family to sleep in one bed, preferably a queen or king size. I didn't take out the garbage to the curb because a waste management service was non-existent.

However, at the tender age of four my father placed a tremendous responsibility on my shoulders. I was assigned to tend our flock of sheep. Just as in the story of Cain and Abel, I was to be the keeper of our sheep. Cain was the tiller of the ground. Perhaps I would have been a better tiller of the ground, since I played in the dirt more often, than learning the nature of those wooly creatures.

So it was, I would wake early in the morning, mount my little white pony and, with the help of our sheep dog, herd the sheep to the pastures to graze. My job was not complete until I returned them all back, safely, into their corral at the end of the day. Readers may recall what kinds of home chores they were doing at the age of four-years-old!

While we children were expected to work hard, we were not deprived from the fun of our childhood years. Just as we worked hard, we also played hard. A favorite game of mine was marbles. It was a simple game, as I remember it. The object of the game was: from a certain distance of the dirt drawn circle, flip your prized marble inside the group of marbles and knock out as many as you could. I don't recall all the rules and penalties, but the one that collected the most marbles was crowned the champ—the marble champ. I believe I won a few of those fierce competitions, but who knows, I could be losing my "marbles."

Another fond memory of mine was pushing a tin wheel with a wooden stick. We would find scraps of tin and shape them into wheels. I got so good at pushing this wheel, I could go over rocks, through water, up and down hills, never letting it fall. It was not a very sophisticated toy, but it provided me with hours of entertainment and fun.

There was one game I had to practice a lot: quarter tossing. However, we did not have any quarters. We had to depend on our most common commodity, tin. That meant we had to form the tin into quarter-sized shapes with the limited tools we had—our hands and rocks. After successfully molding our "quarters," we grabbed our share and met at a designated "tienda" (corner store).

The store had the best walls at which to throw the

"quarters." The challenge was to skillfully toss your "quarters" from approximately seven feet away, towards the wall. The one that could get the "quarters" to land closest to the wall was the winner. The object of the game was, the more games won, the more "quarters" we collected from our opponents. The benefit of this was the less likelihood of having to make more "quarters" on our own.

These were not the only activities I participated in, as a young boy. There were ventures to the nearby river, hikes along the mountains, climbing trees with my buddies, running through rain puddles, playing our version of cowboys and Indians and hide and seek. They are sweet memories that I will forever treasure.

At four years of age, I really had no worries, I had not yet dreamed my big dreams. I had no desire to conquer the highest peak of the Andes Mountains, no ambitions to develop the latest medical miracle pill, no future plans to be the president of Bolivia. Life for me was simple! I was living a wonderful life in a loving environment and in a pleasant home with comfortable surroundings. I considered myself a fortunate boy. These are the blessings every boy and girl should enjoy. And yet, the Lord in His infinite wisdom, knew that in order for me to experience true joy and happiness, beyond my limited understanding, He would have to intervene in my precious life to bring to pass His plans for me.

CHAPTER 2

Destiny Set in Motion

---

*S*ometime during the first week of September 1970, I was visiting my father who was working at the local outdoor sugar cane factory.

"Hola papa," I gestured to my father.

"Hola, mi hijo," he responded, as he stretched his arms to greet me. Our visit was brief, as he went about his business, and I set out to investigate the archaic "candy factory." I wandered for a little while with the curiosity of a child, until I approached the sugarcane press. What was to transpire next, changed the course of my destiny. Or was it destiny that occurred?

My memory is not clear as to exactly how or what happened or the excruciating pain I felt on this particular occasion. But one thing I cannot deny: God was watching over me.

To my young, bewildered eyes, the sugar-cane press seemed enormous in size, and sophisticated in its operation. Compared to the technology of today, it would appear to be a prehistoric dinosaur of a machine. The structure was rather simple—three wooden poles, each ten inches in diameter, standing on a post with rotators, inside a secure frame.

At the top of each pole, grooves were carved, designed to give them grinding capacity, as they rotated. According to my observations, this is where the canes were placed to be crushed. From the top of the wooden frame, two long poles about five inches in diameter and ten feet in length were suspended from the sides. At the end of each pole, a set of oxen was connected with leather straps to provide the power.

The process was simple. As the oxen walked forward, the long poles attached to them would begin to rotate the three grooved columns. The worker next to the press would feed sugar canes into the teeth of the poles. As one can well imagine, this "trapiche" (press), squeezed the canes with tremendous pressure. The sweet juices that were extracted would drip into a collection system which ultimately flowed into a large pool where it was collected for processing.

Observing that no one was working this machine, I approached the pile of sugarcane next to the press. I grasped a stalk and proceeded to place it between the poles. That action immediately signaled the oxen to begin walking forward.

The oxen started to move. The poles started to turn. Little did I realize at the time that my destiny was also being set in motion!

While having a firm hold of the cane, I wasn't prepared to see it actually being crushed. To my amazement, the cane continued to disappear into the maw.

As a little boy of high spirits, I rose to the challenge, hoping to pull it out and prevail in this battle of boy versus machine. Even sooner than I realized what was happening, my right hand was being crushed. At this point I don't recall screaming for help, or for that matter, even thinking about it. Everything was happening so fast!

The next thing I knew, my right arm had been crushed to my elbow. In a desperate effort I desperately placed my left hand on what remained of my right arm and tried to pull it out, but to no avail! I was trapped! Both of my arms were being crushed between the jaws of this press! All my young energy that was surging forward to save me from catastrophe was overwhelmed by blackness and I fainted.

I do not know exactly what happened, immediately after I fainted. However, I vaguely remember being driven in the bed of an old pickup truck to the nearest hospital. The closest town with a hospital was Sucre—almost two hundred miles away. I believe it took nearly a day before we arrived at Santa Barbara Hospital. Keep in mind our primitive conditions: We did not have the convenience of paved roads. Life-flight helicopters or ambulances; 911 systems were non-existent.

Perhaps the most crucial element was the lack of knowledge of basic first-aid. Not even elementary care was given on my behalf to treat my abrasions and serious lacerations. By the time I arrived at the hospital, my entire right arm had become infected with gangrene. There was little, in fact, the doctors could do to save my badly mutilated arm.

The doctors believed there was no choice but to amputate my right arm and shoulder. Removing my entire arm would prevent the infection from contaminating the rest of my body, hopefully, saving me from certain death. The doctors also attempted to mend serious lacerations on my left hand but they could do little to repair the broken bones in my hand.

Often, when I tell people this part of my story, I hear

comments, such as, "If only the workers had been more alert, your accident could have been prevented." Or, "If your accident occurred here, the doctors could have saved your arm." And "Abel, you should have never gotten near that press in the first place!"

I refer to these remarks as the SHUDDAS, CUDDAS, and the WUDDAS of my life.

Hypothetically, none of those things would have occurred IF some kind of intervention had taken place. The fact of the matter is that they *did* happen and there isn't anything I can do but accept them as they are. Why should I waste time and energy on trying to reverse the past? This will not bring comfort or solace to our lives, but only mulch the pain and dull our minds. We must accept the past for what it was, not for what it should have been, could have been, or would have been. We should take comfort in knowing that the Lord has a purpose for each one of us.

With our limited mortal comprehension it is sometimes difficult to understand His infinite wisdom. He controls our destiny. From the very beginning He has governed my life. I am fortunate to have had humble beginnings, for it has taught me to be more submissive. I was blessed with devoted parents who taught me valued principles. I was challenged at an early age with a life-threatening accident. This swung the doors wide open with greater opportunities and countless blessings, more than I could have imagined. And I have just barely begun to relate the wonderful miracles in my life.

So, do I grieve over my past? Absolutely not! Rather, I celebrate them. Do I concentrate on the SHUDDAS, CUDDAS, and WUDDAS of my life? Unequivocally not! Instead, I learn from them. Up to that point in my life at the Santa Barbara Hospital in Bolivia, my life seemed right on course. But now,

I just had to learn how to navigate through it with only one arm.

Some observations I have made with regards to my most traumatic situation: From that moment on, I knew that I would be considered *different* in the eyes of the world.

Whoa! Stop there! *Different*, not *weird*, is good! What if we all looked like Tom Cruise or Cindy Crawford! It would probably be a pretty dull world. (I am not arguing we don't have more room for Cindy clones.)

I joined the ranks and have the designation of being classified *handicapped*, or the more politically correct term, *physically challenged*. Hey, as long as they don't classify me as an UFO (unclassified foolish object) I am comfortable with the handicapped title. Yet, remember, I am still a person, not a category.

Good heavens! At least I still *have* an identity! If I am looked upon, only from the narrow end of the scope, who is responsible for turning that scope around? I am! I will never dress or feed myself the same way as others may. Who cares! As long as I can eat and have clothes to wear. I can't play my games and sports, again, in the same manner. That's right! I know I must just play them smarter. I am sometimes the target of tasteless jokes by insensitive and insecure individuals. That goes with the territory.

The bottom line is that we are the captains of our own ships, stewards of our destinations.

Just as a vessel on the open sea, we will have to sail through calm and stormy waters. We have no control over Mother Nature and what she will strew before our paths. But one thing is certain: we are not given challenges that we cannot bear. As the captain of our ship, each of us determines whether we shall drown or stay afloat.

We are all given the necessary tools and resources to sail our ships. And with courage, determination and hope we can navigate our vessels to shore. We can look over our shoulders and witness that the rains are gone and the storms have ceased. We can see clearly, now. It is going to be a bright, bright sunshiny day!

Look straight ahead! There is nothing but blue skies!

After my surgeries it was determined I would remain at Santa Barbara Hospital somewhat longer than they had anticipated. It was not for medical purposes, however. Rather, no one knew of a home to which they could send me.

The doctors and nurses did not have records of my origin, or who my family might be. Little could be learned about the circumstances of how I arrived at this facility.

They only knew that I was brought there by my mother who was never heard from, again. I can only imagine my parents' sense of helplessness and grief, conveying me to strangers to hopefully, mend and heal their small child.

And so, this hospital, administered by Catholic Nuns, became an oasis in my life. It was to be my home for the following two years.

During those trying childhood years of self-deprecation and despair, I was traumatized most by my physical inability to perform even the simplest of tasks for myself. I could not dress myself. I could not feed myself. I could not even tie my shoe laces.

I found myself confined to a physical body which could no longer care for its own most basic needs. I found that I must rely on the kindness and generosity of other people to do for me the many things I could no longer do for myself. Fortunately, my legs were intact, enabling me to move around and investigate the many things a curious boy may see in his world.

However, I could not help but feel a sense of incompleteness and loneliness that I was sure could never be dissipated during my lifetime. And yet, during those long, but crucial years of my childhood's incapacity, I realize, now, that I was always in the perfect place at the perfect time.

I was always in the company of other children, like myself, who were suffering from seriously debilitating physical problems. Few of these had any hope for recovery.

My entire shoulder and right arm was gone, and my poor, traumatized left arm retained a crushed hand which had never received more than rudimentary medical treatment during those first painful years.

My memories are few of Santa Barbara Hospital. My sleeping quarters were in a ward-like environment, lined with beds and cribs. People of all ages with all types of deformities were treated there. I can remember on one occasion, a truck with a group of people in the back, arriving at the front doors of the hospital. All of them needed medical attention. One particular individual stands out vividly in my mind.

As best as he could, he hopped off the truck, screaming, "Ayuda me. Ayuda me!" (Help me! Help me!) Then, pointing to his swollen leg, from his foot to his thigh, he continued screaming, "I've been bitten by a poisonous snake!"

For a few moments I watched this man in agony. I remember wishing that I could do something for him. It was as if I understood and could feel his pain. Just then, a group of nurses and doctors rushed out and attended to his needs. I don't know what became of that man, but I learned a great lesson from that experience about the quality of compassion.

The man with the snake-bitten leg was truly in pain, and was reaching out for a helping hand. As a bystander, I truly experienced pity and felt sympathetic to his mortal yearning. True compassion is exhibited, when there is a humble heart and a contrite spirit.

Sometimes, the quality of compassion can be misdirected. From my own life, this is an example of that kind of misdirection:

After two years of marriage, I was experiencing financial difficulties, brought on by my own actions. In a desperate effort to extract us from our financial difficulties, I devised a devious plan. I told my wife that I had just spoken on the telephone with a friend of mine in Los Angeles, California.

I compounded that lie by telling her that my friend was willing to give us the money necessary to relieve our problems. All I needed to do, was to travel to his home and pick up the money. She was hesitant and bewildered with that strategy, but she went along with my plan.

Keep in mind that this contrived plan was actually far-removed from my actual plans. It was simply the subterfuge I used in order to carry out my deception.

Somehow, I scraped together enough money to purchase a round-trip airline ticket to Los Angeles, California, arriving early on a Friday morning. I boarded a bus to Beverly Hills and found myself in the business district at about nine a.m.

I walked to the nearest store, purchased a neon orange poster-board and a black marker and some string. I tied the string at one end of the poster board so that I could wear it around my neck.

I proceeded to write on the poster board in big letters,

"PLEASE GIVE ME A HAND."

My whole intention with this strategy, of course, was to garner some pity and emotion, and to elicit compassion from those who saw my sign. With this in mind, I walked to the corner of Wilshire Boulevard and Rodeo Drive. I thought this would be the ideal place to get attention from those with deep pockets, driving in their limousines, Rolls Royces, and Ferraris.

Regardless of the fact that I needed money to get me out of my own mess, I intended to make people feel sorry for me. I wanted people to associate the sign hanging from my neck with my physical appearance.

I really did know better than to undertake such a charade. I truly had been taught better than to do such a thing. I wasn't looking for true compassion with a contrite spirit. I was seeking pity, selfish clemency. I was actually prostituting myself!

It certainly was not a prudent, nor an honorable way to resolve my financial predicament.

Nevertheless, I was determined. I stood on that Beverly Hills corner for nine hours, straight. Not a single soul stopped or paid any attention to my pathetic supplications.

Perhaps, the Lord was punishing me for my errant behavior. Maybe those Beverly Hill types were too preoccupied in their own little worlds to even notice me. In any event, at the end of the day I dragged myself back home to my wife, deeply ashamed of my shabby conduct.

She, sympathetically and magnanimously, accepted my apologies, and we eventually resolved our financial crisis through our own efforts, the way we should have done in it the first place.

A more humorous recollection of mine at Santa Barbara

Hospital occurred on a cold and stormy night. It was thundering so loud, it woke me from my precious sleep. I stood up in my crib, crying and somewhat disillusioned. However, my cries could not be heard by the nuns, sleeping soundly, just across the outside patio, because they were overshadowed by the pounding of the heavy rain.

I was so frightened, I managed to crawl out of my crib to find comfort with one of the nuns. I frantically walked through the patio and reached the nuns' dormitory.

Drenched from the pouring rain, I carefully walked to the nearest bed and noticed a shirt at the foot of the bed. I removed my soaked clothes and placed the warm, dry shirt on my chilled, diminished body. I then proceeded to get under the covers and assumed fetal position with my back snuggled up next to the nun.

The following morning the nun was astonished to see me, comfortably asleep in her bed. Years later, now, I can jokingly say I once slept with a nun.

It is evident from my given name, Abel, that my parents must have been somewhat religious. We first learn of the name Abel in the book of Genesis from which, I assume, my parents derived my name. I can not assume they belonged to a particular faith. Nonetheless, I felt blessed by the influence of God in their lives.

In an unorganized kind of way I was bestowed and privileged with a religious heritage. That bestowal was present while I was staying at Santa Barbara Hospital.

Because that hospital was administered by a Catholic diocese, the patients were often given the opportunity to attend Mass at the nearby church.

I often found myself sitting on the hard pews, reverently observing the altar-server, dressed in his white alb garment, carrying out his assignment of incensing the entrance to the chapel. My eyes also focused on the Holy Communion, so sacredly administered by the priest.

Members lined up to partake of the consecrated bread and wine in remembrance of the body and blood of Christ.

At age six I did not understand the prayers and sermons offered; however, I felt a yearning to partake of the sacrament and share in the spirit of Christ. These elementary beliefs and sentimental feelings would become the foundation of my future relationship with God and His Son, Jesus Christ.

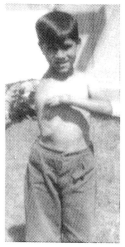

Just when I had resigned myself to the fact that Santa Barbara Hospital had become my home and that the nurses, doctors, and patients would be my family, I was told that I would be transferred to another hospital. My experiences at this hospital lasted approximately two years.

It was deemed necessary to transfer me to a more modern facility for medical purposes. I was now approximately six-years-old. Everyone at the Santa Barbara Hospital had gone out of their way to make me feel comfortable, cared for, and loved. I will ever be grateful for their generosity. In my mind they played an important role in my rearing, particularly at that very critical age in my life.

CHAPTER 3

Children's Center

*M*y destiny led me to Obrajes Children's Rehabilitation Center in La Paz, Bolivia, two hundred miles from Sucre on March 4, 1972. This center housed several children, plagued with nearly every kind of deformity. For most, this was the last stop—a kind of final oasis in the desert, where the children hoped to find magic water that would miraculously restore sight or limbs or the ability to walk.

But when, of course, such miracles didn't happen, despite all the doctor's best efforts, they then were returned to their parents or, too often, turned over to an orphanage. I did not know at the time that this strange place, at first so large and lonely, but ultimately, so filled with love, would become my home for the next four years.

The architectural design of this center was simple. It was a one-level, U-shaped building. The south wing constituted the sleeping quarters for the boys, and the north wing housed the girls. Rows of beds along the walls adorned these dormitories. In the middle portion of the center was the kitchen and dining room. This also served as the main gathering place for games and watching television. I watched some of my favorite shows on a thirteen-inch, black and white, fuzzy screen television that sat on an old dresser in a corner of the dining room.

I can well remember being fascinated with Godzilla, entertained with Zorro, and intrigued with Rin Tin Tin. I had heard that in other countries, especially in America, one could see these programs in living color! I was fascinated with this concept. I hoped that some day I could watch my favorite shows on a color television.

Incredibly, that dream one day would come true for me.

Just outside the rear of the dining room was a laundry facility. It was, mainly, a big masonry washing basin in the middle of the yard where all the laundry was washed by hand. Between the fenced-off hospital and the mountains ran a wide, muddy river. Just east of the sleeping quarters were the operating units and doctors' offices. Several surgeries on my left hand were performed there. South of the boys' wing lay the soccer field, where games were played in wheelchairs, on crutches, stretchers and in casts.

Nothing could prevent us from playing our favorite sport. Our physical limitations only challenged our abilities to dream up ingenious methods to give us an advantage in our games. We always chose as our goalie a kid on a stretcher. That gave us a broader, wider, more horizontal protection against goals.

Of course, our forwards had to be in casts. Nobody likes to be kicked with a hard, solid cast! Our defense needed to be on crutches. Just in case our opponents got a little ahead of us, we had the crutches to slow them with an "accidental" tripping. Even though we played the game for fun, we also played it competitively.

Just south of the soccer field was a good-sized garden, filled with rows of corn, potatoes, peas, tomatoes, and hot peppers. I became good friends with the gardener, Señor Gillermo. I often found myself by his side, helping him pull weeds in the garden or trimming the bushes and shrubbery that lined the hospital.

I remember him being very meticulous with his work. The flowers always seemed to be in full bloom with his expert care. The hedges stood trimmed and the trees were always pruned to perfection. He always took great pride in his work. I suppose that is why his memory stands out so vividly in my mind.

Another hard worker was an elderly woman, Doña Modesta. Her responsibility was to hand-wash all the clothes and bed sheets of the boys and girls. She gathered water in buckets from the nearby river, carried them back to the hospital, and emptied them in the masonry basin.

She then scrubbed the clothes, individually, with a bar of soap. To rinse them off she had to drain the dirty water, and refill it again with river water. Once cleaned, she hung them on stretched wires to dry. She did this from sun-up to sun-down, day in and day out.

I could never forget Manta Pocha. I believe I used to refer to her as, Mama Pocha. She was responsible for keeping me fed, as the main cook for the children. I looked forward to her meals. I always asked for seconds, even though I didn't always get it, because there usually was just enough for one serving per child.

Not only was Mama Pocha a good cook, she was also a great mentor.

She always seemed to be considerate of my needs, by either giving me a little extra helping on my plate, greeting me with a smile, or simply sitting and talking to me at the dinner table. She was not the only one who treated me with such kindness. All the doctors, nurses, and caretakers displayed this type of loving attention, the kind of subsistence I needed during my younger years.

At Obrajes Children's Center I enjoyed some great friends, who, in some ways, shared many physical challenges like mine. And when I say great friends, I mean spiritual giants. For no sooner than I arrived there, they instantly made me feel welcome, as though we had been soul-mates forever.

Macaria Flores had suffered an injury to her legs from her waist down. I do not know exactly the cause of her injuries, but she was unable to stand or sit. She would get around in a bed/cart just two feet off the ground. While lying down on her stomach and, with relative ease, she pulled or pushed herself around with her hands. Macaria was a pretty girl. She wore her hair in braided pony tails. She always had a smile on her face.

All the boys were fond of her smile, myself, included. In fact, she was the first girl I had an innocent boyhood crush on. Not only was she pretty, she was smart. On several occasions she came to my rescue with my spelling and vocabulary assignments. Macaria was someone you could always count on to lift you up when you were feeling down.

Avelino Andrade was bed-ridden with a debilitating bone disease. Because of this condition, he was unable to participate in the outside activities as, I am sure he would like to have done. However, this did not keep him from trying.

He asked the nurses to wheel him out in his bed, so he could at least enjoy the sun and watch our frolicking behavior. Avelino and I, somehow, became very close friends. He was a little older than I, and he became like an older brother. We would talk for hours about anything, and for the most part, our conversations led to laughter.

During my four-year stay at this center, I developed a great respect for Avelino's uncanny example. What led me to my appreciation for this friend of my mine was the devotion and conviction he possessed for his religious beliefs. One of his beliefs was to abstain from harmful substances, such as alcohol, coffee and illicit drugs.

He had explained this to me in a sincere and non-critical approach. Traditionally, one of those items was fed to us on a daily basis at the Center: coffee.

With every meal we were given coffee to drink. I mean the fresh stuff! Brewed every morning from fresh coffee beans. It was potent! And I loved it! Ironically, Avelino never cared to drink a drop of it! This, of course, opened up opportunities for ridicule and mocking by a few of the kids, including myself. At the time, I could not understand why he would not partake of something so addicting and so delicious.

Every time I would tempt him with a cup of coffee, he graciously declined. He never responded with a condescending attitude, or judgmentally lectured that I was going to die and go to Hell for drinking the stuff. Rather, he advanced his philosophy by encouraging me in a loving way to stop drinking coffee.

He promised me that if I did, I could walk and not faint; run and not be weary, something I found rather ironic, coming from someone who must always remain in bed. I never realized then that, years later, I would take on those same beliefs to which Avelino was so firmly committed.

Avelino passed away quietly, one day, at the children's center. The world never knew of his grand courage, his dauntless character, his remarkable approach to life, and his belief in God.

But I did!

He left a tremendous impact on my life. He was never weary in well-doing. He laid the foundation of a great work. A long time ago, he planted the seeds in my heart of what being an example for good, truly means. From small things proceedeth great and marvelous things!

Sometime in 1974, when I was approximately eight-years-old, Mary Oleson, a resident of Maryland, of the United States, began volunteering her time every Friday at the Center. Her husband had been named director of the USAID project to Bolivia in September of 1973. USAID is the United States Agency for International Development. Their primary focus in Bolivia was health, agriculture and education.

That good-will assignment in the district of Cochabamba in Bolivia opened a window of opportunity for Mary. She was invited to visit our facility by a social worker. After this experience, she committed herself to do valuable service for the children at the Center. From the very first visit, with her elementary-aged son, Erik, Mary stretched forth her loving arms and extended her benevolent heart in an altruistic fashion to all the children at the Center.

For some reason, she took a particular interest in my life. Her ultimate compassion for my welfare led me to address her as "Tia" Mary: Aunt Mary. That salutation came to symbolize that she was not just another face in my life, but someone whom I claimed to be a part of me: a family member. One of my fondest memories of Tia Mary took place during the Christmas season.

It was a week before Christmas, 1975 at the Children's

Rehabilitation Center in La Paz, Bolivia. Preparations were being made for this joyous occasion. Everyone seemed to be in the Christmas Spirit. The doctors, nurses, cooks, gardeners, boys and girls, all pitched in to make this a Christmas to remember! We trimmed the tree with homemade decorations, paper-made snowflakes and a paper-chain garland. The kitchen help assisted us in cooking some appetizers, our favorites: beef empanadas and churos. The gardeners put some finishing touches on the dining room where the Christmas tree stood tall, glittering with festive charm.

That same evening we held a "fiesta." As I mentioned, the common beverage served was coffee to compliment the savory homemade scones. We sang our favorite Christmas jingles: "Feliz Navidad," "Noche de Paz," "Jingle Bells." We awkwardly danced, to the best of our abilities, to the beat of folkloric music. The party reached its high point, when each of the kids, those that could, got to sit on Santa's lap. I waited, patiently, for my turn. I knew exactly what I wanted to ask for—a yellow truck.

Once on Santa's lap, I whispered in his ear what I wanted him to bring me for Christmas.

The week seemed to last forever! "When will Christmas be here?!" I thought to myself. All week long, in my little boy's mind, I imagined playing with my new truck.

Much sooner than I realized, Christmas morning had arrived. All the kids in the Center were lined up, single file, still dressed in our scraggly pajamas. We reverently sang "Noche de Paz, Noche de Luz" as we quietly marched to where our gifts awaited us. Upon entering the dining room, I could not believe my eyes! Gifts of all sizes covered the floor around the Christmas tree.

"I wonder which one is mine," I whispered to my friend.

Tia Mary was in charge of handing out the gifts. As we sat on the floor, she called out our names to let us know when to come up and get our gift. Several kids were called up before I was. Then, Tia Mary picked up a gift the size of a shoe box and said, "I wonder whose this is?"

Playfully, she looked at the tag and said, "Abelito!" I leaped from the floor and hurriedly made my way to Tia Mary. She handed me the gift, gave me a kiss on my cheek and said, "Feliz Navidad."

I looked, immediately, for a place on the dining room floor, where I could open my Christmas surprise. I placed the gift between my knees and began to tear the newspaper wrapping with my tattered hand, hoping that I would find a truck underneath all the paper. After removing the lid from the box, I looked inside to discover the most wonderful gift in the whole wide world: a bright, yellow truck!

There was nothing exotic about the truck. It did not make any amazing noises. It did not have any pin-striping. It was not made from sturdy material. It was a simple truck made out of plastic. For me, it was perfect!

Even though I was a young boy, I recognized the generosity rendered by whoever made this small miracle come true for me. Tears began to roll down my face as I whispered to myself, "Gracias, Gracias." Later on in my life, I learned that my beloved Tia Mary was the giver of the great joy on that memorable Christmas day.

Tia Mary, in the simplest terms, was my protagonist. Her warm presence, every Friday at the Center, provided me with the comfort and the security of a loved one. To this very day, Tia Mary's presence remains with me as we continue our special friendship via U.S. mail and, sometimes, electronic mail. Whenever I think of gifts given and gifts received, I think of Tia Mary, the giver of love!

I have introduced here only a few of the individuals who played a significant role during a crucial time in my life at the Center. Without regard for themselves, doctors and patients, nurses and gardeners, maids and maidens, all generously gave of themselves on my behalf. Their fervent love and concern gave me the hope and the courage I needed to endure my daunting challenges without bitterness.

But, of all of those persons whose kind and tender feelings and actions had blessed my life so abundantly, none would become such a miraculous instrument in shaping my future as was Luz Bustamante.

CHAPTER 4

Luz Bustamante—
"Miracle Worker"

---

*L*et me first preface this chapter, by describing my emotional state during my first year at the Children's Center. It had started to dawn on my young, six year old consciousness that I yearned for my family. I hadn't seen them since my accident! Naturally, I began to develop questions in my mind: "Where were they?" "Why hadn't they visited me?" "Did they know where I was?" "What was to become of me?"

While I was suffering, emotionally and physically, my parents, I'm certain, were also experiencing pain at the deepest personal levels. It was years later that I experienced an anxiety similar to what my parents must have been going through.

As parents, ourselves, my wife, Wendy and I experienced the pain one feels when their child is in crisis. Only eight-days-old in this world, our beautiful son, Johvan, developed a blockage, due to malrotation of his bowels. His large intestine had become twisted. Food was unable to pass through his digestive system.

That effect caused symptoms of projectile vomiting, leaving

him weak and quivering. After witnessing several of these attacks, we realized Johvan's life was in danger. Being new and inexperienced parents we were afraid and felt somewhat confused as to what to do for him.

Fortunately, we took Johvan to his pediatrician who performed tests, and concluded that we needed to take him directly to the emergency room at Primary Children's Medical Center near our home in Salt Lake City. After several more tests and examinations the doctors confirmed that Johvan was in critical need of medical intervention. We embraced each other and cried as the doctors took our new born baby boy in their arms and disappeared through the doors labeled, "Operating Room."

We sat in the waiting room, for hours that seemed forever, with prayers in our hearts, hoping everything would turn out all right. As difficult as it was to accept, we had done everything within our power to take care of his needs. It was crucial that we allow the Lord and the doctors to intervene on our baby's behalf. He was now in their hands! We were blessed to have our prayers answered. Johvan recovered and is a strong little boy, today.

In a similar crucial circumstance, what else could my own parents have done? The nature of my injury was something which they had never experienced before. With their limited understanding they did everything possible to save my life.

Because of their meager resources, they made a decision on my behalf, a very difficult choice, to deliver me to the doctors and nurses at the nearest hospital to tend to my needs and to do their best to heal my broken body. So, in answering the questions I posed to myself, I realized my parents did not have the means, financially or materially, to make the journey to visit me. We were several hundred miles apart!

They could not leave the farm or the animals unattended! To have left the farm, even briefly, could have meant economic ruin for the whole family. That was their livelihood. So, just as Wendy and I did, they depended on a higher power to ease their concerns and soothe their fears. With that certainty alone, even to this day, I am confident that they did the right thing, and they knew I was in good hands.

I love my parents, dearly. I understand and can never regret the choice they made for me. As difficult as it must have been to give me up, they made the right choice. I am also grateful to them for giving me life and the chance to become a part of this world and to participate in its opportunities and challenges.

For the very essence of life, fully and maturely lived, is *challenge*. If this were not so, we would never be called upon to lift ourselves to greater heights and develop, constantly develop, into something greater. The significant life is not about avoiding trouble or finding fast and easy pleasures. Rather, it is about creatively and courageously confronting adversity in order to grow.

The choices we make in life, good or bad, will determine the progress of our growth and, ultimately, the quality of our future. But remember, these are *our choices*—choices by which each of us, like an artist, will paint our own self-portrait—the picture of our life. The great philosopher, Nikos Kazantakis said it well:

> *"You have your brush, you have your colors; you paint paradise, then, in you go. And if you want to paint hell, go ahead and paint it, but then don't blame me, and don't blame your parents and don't blame society. And for goodness sake, don't blame God. You must take full responsibility for creating your own hell."*

One of my favorite television commercials is a scene of a little boy and girl, sitting next to each other on the front steps of a home. The little boy turns toward the little girl and offers her a *Lifesaver Candy* as a wedding ring. The narrator then says, "Isn't life delicious?" Paint the wrong picture, and life will always be bitter. But paint the right picture and, with me, you'll agree: Isn't life delicious?

Without parents, I was left to envy the laughter, hugs and kisses that other children shared with their families. It was sometimes difficult to hold my emotions inside, but I found myself, sometimes, sitting next to the tall tree adjacent to the hospital, weeping, reaching out for attention.

Now, as surely as the sun rises, my childish cries did not go unnoticed. For when I was about six-years-old, I crossed paths with Luz Bustamante. She was a marvelous woman with the grandeur of Mother Theresa, caring in every way. She seemed to breathe and exhale compassion. At age seventy-six, her black hair still maintained a youthful softness. Her dark brown eyes transmitted a glimmer of hope.

Her dazzling smile sparked a glimmer of love. The name "Luz" in Spanish translates to "light." And the Lord, being aware of my needs, sent me an angel of light! For the following four years she was my guiding light, my pillar of devotion, my reservoir of love.

I can scarcely do justice to the joy of explaining who Luz was and what she meant to me, but what I hope to accomplish is to pierce your hearts and let you feel the intensity of her compassionate character. For in my eyes, she was not only a social worker, she was a miracle-worker, a valiant servant of God.

I know little of her background, family, home, or culture.

Perhaps, those things are of no importance in the grand scale of things, and it is sometimes best to leave it at that. My memories of her unselfish service to me shall forever illuminate my life!

Interestingly enough, Luz began volunteering at the Children's Center at almost the same time I arrived there. From the very beginning of my stay at the center, Luz affectionately began exercising her role as my mother figure. That mantle seemed altogether natural to Luz. Small things she did made me feel like I was one of her own children. She referred to me as her little "Abelito."

She constantly encouraged and complemented me on the way I managed and handled myself with only one arm. Sometimes, Luz gave me money to buy treats at the "tienda" near the Center for all the children. Her only reward for doing this simple act of kindness was watching the smiles on our faces as we eagerly opened the wrappers of the "Chicklets" or "Bazooka" gum. Little by little, line upon line, precept upon precept, Luz was teaching me lessons of self-respect and confidence, traits I have found valuable through my later years.

As our special relationship matured, Luz felt confident she could share with me concerns she had been thinking about for some time. When I was about eight-years-old, she told me that she was very impressed with how adept I had become in using my deformed hand. However, Luz said she felt something more could be done to make it more useful to me. She envisioned the possibility of additional surgeries on my left hand—this time performed by a hand specialist who could perform corrective surgery so that I might once again regain mobility in my hand.

Luz also wanted to see me fitted with a prosthetic limb to, somehow, replace my missing right arm. Luz revealed that she had arranged for the two of us to travel to Buenos Aires, Argentina, to consult with a hand surgeon who would, hopefully, fulfill Luz's dreams for me. Needless to say, I was ecstatic with the upcoming trip and the exciting possibilities it represented.

Several weeks later, with Luz by my side, we visited a doctor in Argentina. After several days of examinations, studies, and tests, it was determined that the doctor could not provide the prosthetic help which I needed.

"I am very sorry, young man, but I am unable to help you."

Deeply disappointed, Luz and I packed our bags and returned to the children's center.

Two more years passed before the most significant journey of my life would take place. Determined to save me from the plight of my eventually being sent to an orphanage, Luz graciously made travel arrangements for me to fly to Salt Lake City, Utah, where I could, finally, receive expert medical treatment.

Before describing my trip to Salt Lake City, I find it necessary to recount the tremendous struggle Luz went through to make this dream a reality for me, an extraordinary effort which I did not fully comprehend, until just recently. In my possession, I have a few documents, letters, and records that explain Luz's correspondence with various people in Bolivia and Utah. Because I was deemed orphaned, I was legally in the custody of the Bolivian Government under the jurisdiction of the National Council for Children.

I was amazed to learn the details of the difficult endeavors she went through in order to slash through all the bureaucratic red tape. All that effort, in order that she might realize her dream for a small Bolivian orphan boy! She made numerous telephone calls, and wrote a myriad of letters to various government agencies, just to get approval for me to leave the country.

She even went as far as to personally speak to the president of the Republic of Bolivia in order to get permission to let me leave the children's center. After much consideration and delay, they granted her request. I cannot begin to mention all of the people involved with my case, but nevertheless, there were many people who played an important role in gaining permission for me to leave Bolivia.

Sometime in the late sixties or early seventies, a program was developed by the United States Government called Alliance For Progress. The purpose was to create a partnership between the United States Government and South American Governments. From this entity the Partners of America was created. Only a few states participated in this program, and Utah happened to be one of them. The State of Utah became a partner to Bolivia.

Mr. Boyd Wenegren, a professor at Utah State University, in Logan, Utah, became actively involved with this project. Wenegren made several trips to La Paz to children's hospitals and orphanages on a kind of "scouting" mission. After evaluating conditions, circumstances and needs of some of the children from various facilities, he would make recommendations to those administrations on how best to apply for help.

I was one of those fortunate children. He recommended to Luz that she apply to the Shriners Hospital in Salt Lake City, Utah, for intervening medical treatment. In early 1974, Luz did just that.

Another individual whom Luz made contact with on my behalf was Dr. Andrew W. Peterson. While serving as a member of the Utah-Bolivia Partner program, Dr. Peterson, a dentist, in May of 1975, traveled to La Paz with his wife, Chris, to visit and evaluate conditions of several orphanages and to offer his services to the children. They were also seeking to adopt a child. They fell in love with a baby boy at the Carlos de Viegas orphanage. Part of the adoption process was for the Petersons to appear before the orphanage board to receive final approval.

Luz Bustamante was a member of that board, and, thereby, became acquainted with Dr. Peterson. In connection with that adoption experience, throughout the next two years, Dr. Peterson made several trips back to La Paz, and assisted others in Utah with their adoption efforts. Each time, Luz was instrumental in completing the various adoptions. Because Luz and Dr. Peterson had established a mutual association, Luz found the opportunity to request a helping hand from Dr. Peterson to advance her efforts on my behalf.

After several phone calls and letters from Luz to Dr. Peterson, he became sympathetic to her requests and kindly agreed to use his good offices in advancing her request. After some correspondence, it was arranged for me to be taken to the Shriners Hospital in Salt Lake City, Utah.

It was suggested and agreed that Dr. Peterson would become my legal guardian when I arrived in Salt Lake City, Utah. However, Luz's ultimate dream was for a family to adopt me and save me from eventually being sent to an orphanage. The following are translated excerpts from a letter written by Luz Bustamante to Dr. Andrew Peterson, dated June 30, 1976, just a few days before I left the Center:

> *"My dream is that somehow you could find a couple that will adopt him, realizing this to be a challenge and somewhat difficult, but nonetheless a caring couple that can give him a*

*pleasant home after he leaves Shriners Hospital.
I hate to think that after all our efforts, his trip
to Utah would be fruitless if this is were not
realized."*

Then, Luz adds in one of her final paragraphs:

*"Dr. Peterson, my last favor: for the past four
years I've taken care of him like my own son. I
feel very close to him. As long as I am alive, I
want to know everything about him, I do not
want to lose contact with him."*

One can understand the emotions Luz must have been
feeling while expressing her feelings to Dr. Peterson. It was as
if she had exhausted all her options, and this was my last hope
to receive proper medical care and to live what remained of my
"normal" childhood life, in a loving home. Luz did in four
short years what some parents are not willing to do in their
lifetimes for their children; to nurture, care and provide
opportunities, so that some day they may do likewise, creating
a cycle of absolute love.

I would be most ungrateful if I did not recognize the fact
that I benefitted, directly, and in so many important ways from
Luz's efforts. Even more than the concrete advantages I gained
from her exertions for me, was something intangible. For what
I finally received from Luz at the deepest personal level was an
example of what it means to never desert or even diminish your
dreams. That lesson has served me well. A person, near and
dear to me, once told me, "Abel, the problem with you is that
you are a dreamer!"

But you see, that is not the problem in me; that is the power
in me and in each of us—the power to pursue a dream; the same
power that led Christopher Columbus to discover this great

country of ours; the same force that drove our founding fathers to create this free and wonderful nation; the same energy that led Benjamin Franklin to discover electricity and Thomas Edison to discover the light bulb; the same power that drove Luz, despite many discouragements and seeming impossibilities, to follow her vision. So I ask you to share that dream with me:

I have a Dream,
People across this nation
Embrace your creation
In one great dance of celebration

I have a Dream,
World leaders, together
Stop world wars forever
Peace and harmony is better

I have a Dream,
Voices, praise liberty
Proclaim death of bigotry.
I like the sound of that melody

I have a Dream,
Rulers, dictators and kings
Remove your violent stings
Govern by the hand of The Supreme

I have a Dream,
Pull the thorns of greed
From every race, color and creed
We plant instead, loves seed

This is my final Dream:
People linked in hope and trust,
Joined in a world, tender and just,
Where love and laughter reign supreme!

The key to unlock this door of your dreams (which otherwise will remain forever barred) is *effort*. The great Chen Tu-Obu once remarked, *"Man's happiness in life is the result of man's own effort, and is neither the gift of God, nor a spontaneous natural product. "*

It is interesting to me that Adam and Eve were cast out of the Garden of Eden to experience that same principle. They would never have been able to conceptually grasp the idea of good and evil, right and wrong, virtue and vice, had they not lifted that first finger and began the process of "struggle" by the sweat of their brows.

Effort becomes a teaching experience, only when it begins to hurt. I am reminded often of this axiom as I reflect upon my life, where I was many years ago and where I am now. It is all because of a single woman's efforts. For Luz, effort was a satisfying struggle by which she attained a goal—a more meaningful, productive life for me.

One of the issues Luz had to resolve before I left the Center was to present the government with my birth certificate, showing the date of my birth. In fact, I had no such document. She wrote several letters to Santa Barbara Hospital, requesting any documentation of my birth, but she received no response.

Rather than pursuing a dead-end road, Luz creatively came up with a clever and loving solution. She knew that the only information missing on my birth document was an official date of birth. She needed to find a date reserved for me. But it could not be just any birth date, it needed to be a date with profound significance.

Luz Bustamante

Luz offered me the tender token of her love by endowing me with her birth date, February 3rd. That date symbolizes the rewards of hard work and perseverance by a magnificent lady! That date signifies that the power of love and the influence of service can, and will, benefit society to change our habits of selfishness! That date clearly states that, yes, one person can make a difference! And so, it has always seemed appropriate to me each year, as I celebrate my (our) birth date, that I, also, celebrate life! A life, perhaps I wouldn't have celebrated, had it not been for Luz's unremitting kindness.

While Luz was busily putting things together for my trip, I

did not have the faintest idea that I was about to embark on the journey of my life! Several weeks before my departure, Luz took me aside to reveal the exciting news. She placed her gentle hand on my shoulder, looked into my eyes, and enthusiastically said, "Abelito, te vas para America!" (You are going to America!)

"America?" I inquisitively responded. I vaguely knew where America was: where all the movie stars lived with big homes, nice cars and fancy clothes that I had come to know through the magic of television. Luz continued, by telling me when I would be leaving and the other details that boggled my mind, as I drifted into oblivion, thinking only of "America."

After I emerged from my Hollywood dream state, Luz and I both hugged each other tightly, not letting go for several seconds. Tears began to roll down our faces, as we realized that our fervent dream had become a reality. Luz's persistent efforts had borne magnificent fruit!

During my remaining days at the Center, I passed my good news to everyone. They shared in the same excitement I was feeling, for we were all aware such an opportunity is seldom, if ever, realized. Then, I realized I would be leaving them—the kind nurses, gardeners, doctors, and my little confidants who had become like family to me over the past four years. I was leaving my native country for a strange land. I was leaving behind familiar faces to find strange people with strange "food."

Somehow, though, they all reassured me everything would be all right; their thoughts and prayers would be with me at all times. To demonstrate their love and enthusiasm for me, the evening before I boarded the plane to leave, the kids and hospital staff threw a farewell party in my honor. The kitchen area was decorated with balloons, and hand-made decorations, banners and posters. We celebrated with song and dance to the tune of familiar Andean music.

My farewell party was capped with each child, wishing me well on my journey, and assuring me I would be missed. Some showered me with gifts with which to remember them, such as a leather wallet, a wool hat, small wooden figurines and some money, each individually selected. I knew full well these were sometimes their only and most prized possessions.

Others handed notes and letters to me to read on the plane. Even though each one wrote that they would miss me, not one expressed their envy, hoping that they might be the ones leaving, instead of me, or that they were unhappy with the circumstances. Rather, each page was filled with words of encouragement and love, reinforcing the fact that I was very fortunate and blessed to be experiencing this once-in-a-lifetime opportunity. The evening finally came to an end, bringing to a close a memorable chapter of my life in Bolivia and the beginning of a brand new adventure in America.

CHAPTER 5

Leaving La Paz

---

*T*he anticipation of the coming events left me sleepless that evening before the flight. But sooner than I expected, the morning sun was peeking through the windows of the dormitory, one last time for me, on July 1, 1976.

Luz, with a broad smile on her face, greeted me at the front entrance of the Center. We gathered the few belongings I had, and together, we walked solemnly toward the waiting taxi. Our pensive mood continued, as we made our way to the airport. I don't believe we spoke a word to each other en route. The atmosphere we had created was stronger than any word we could say to each other. Somehow, we both understood the emotions we were experiencing and wanted to cherish them for as long as possible. We knew we had reached the moment, when we would have to part and say goodby. While she gently held my tattered hand, Luz and I gazed out the car window basking in the fond memories of four wonderful years together.

The taxi came to a stop at the airline terminal curve. Luz

motioned to the driver to wait for her while she helped me with my luggage. We walked toward the ticket booth where I received the airline ticket and instructions by the attending agent. Soon after, Luz took me aside, gave me a hug, placed a kiss on my forehead and tearfully told me, "Te amo." (I love you.) She then walked toward the taxi and drove away.

Just then, a young lady greeted me, "Hola, soy Hermana Watson." (Hi, I'm Sister Watson.) She was a missionary for The Church of Jesus Christ of Latter-day Saints, returning home to America. Luz had made arrangements for Sister Watson to be my temporary guardian during my flight.

My not seeing Luz again seemed unimaginable. Was this really the way our friendship was going to end? Luz staying behind, and I, moving on without her? Four years of faithfully being there for me had come to a conclusion, or so I believed.

Almost one year into my life in America, Luz paid me a surprise visit. It was a wonderful reunion filled with hugs and kisses and reminiscing. Also, every Christmas during my first three years in America, I joyfully received letters that Luz faithfully wrote. Each was filled with encouragement and love. Without fail she reminded me of how fortunate I was and counseled me, "Don't always be a receiver of gifts. Be a giver of gifts and you'll get back ten-fold."

Luz lived that principle until the day her weary body was laid to rest sometime in 1981. Everyone who was touched by Luz, especially the children at the Center in Bolivia, lost a truly spiritual giant, but the heavens gained a divine angel.

I am confident she carries on her mission, as a saint. All who knew her miss her, dearly, but her wonderful smile, her gentle voice, and her enduring love remains in our hearts, always. Even though Luz is not physically by my side, her spirit continues fervently within me, breathing and exuding compassion.

With Sister Watson by my side, I slowly walked up the portable stairs to the airplane being fueled, preparing for take-off. Several media personnel from local newspapers surrounded the bottom of the stairs with cameras to their faces, screaming for my attention. I did not understand it all: the pictures, the questions, all the attention. A couple of days later, a small article with my picture appeared in one of the major newspapers (forwarded to me by Tia Mary) briefly explaining my years in hospitals and the successful efforts of Luz in getting me to America.

Today, I am not surprised to know that word got out to the rest of the world of the simple miracles that were being quietly performed by Luz Bustamante at the Children's Center in La Paz, Bolivia.

Once in the cabin of the plane, we made our way to our assigned seats. I sat by the window and Sister Watson sat next to me on the aisle seat. My previous and only other flight experience was to Argentina. For some reason this trip was going to be different. I could hardly wait!

Over the intercom, the captain welcomed us aboard and asked us to fasten our seat belts, secure our seats in an upright position, return the trays to their proper position, and extinguish all cigarettes.

We were ready for take off! The flight attendants all decked out in their neatly pressed uniforms, instructed us in some safety measures: where to locate oxygen masks and inflatable life preservers (we were flying overseas), pointing out the emergency doors and windows, and some other things that didn't register with me. Soon after, I heard the engines whistling loudly. Then slowly, the plane began taxiing to the runway.

Moments later, to my surprise, the plane picked up speed, a lot of speed, when suddenly the nose of the plane lifted upward. I looked out the window and noticed that, by now, the whole plane was off the ground. I swallowed hard, enveloped in the strange sensation I was feeling. It was as if the weight of my body was being forced to stay in the seat while another part of me was being elevated. For a moment I didn't know if I could hold down my food, but somehow I managed.

I remember the flight as being long and tiring. On top of that, I felt bloated and uncomfortable (I did not realize these planes were outfitted with bathrooms). So, as you may well imagine, I tried to sit and suffer in silence so that Sister Watson, sitting next to me, would remain ignorant of my predicament.

Needless to say, I was relieved when the plane finally landed at the Los Angeles, California Airport. Even with the occasional motion sickness and stomach pains, my flight experience was interesting, to say the least, for this ten-year-old, one-time Bolivian shepherd boy. Besides, where else can you eat an unlimited amount of peanuts for nine hours straight?

My layover in Los Angeles seemed to last for hours. In actuality it was barely enough time to walk from the landing terminal to my departing terminal. It was a good thing Sister Watson was with me, because I would have become lost in the maze of terminals, gates, and thousands of people.

I was in awe at everything I saw. Everything seemed big, elaborate and sophisticated. It was like I was coming out of a shell, from seclusion, from being sheltered, to find that there was a larger life beyond my youthful years at the Children's Center.

My only exposure to that type of environment was from the programs I used to watch on television. But those were only fantasies and fictitious characters. Here I was, at the Los Angeles Airport, the Mecca of America, thousands of miles away from home, breathing the stale air and seeing with my own eyes the images that until now had been figments of my imagination.

After taking in the sights and sounds of the Los Angeles Airport, I once again boarded another airplane. Its destination: Salt Lake City, Utah. We landed sometime in the morning of July 2, 1976. I believe that during that leg of the flight I was without the accompaniment of Sister Watson, since her home was in Los Angeles.

Not to worry though, everything was under control. Luz had made arrangements for someone from Shriners Hospital to pick me up at the gate, and, as planned, someone there greeted me with open arms. After we gathered my belongings at the luggage return, we walked to the awaiting van and drove to Shriners Hospital.

Shriners Hospital is located in the Avenues of the northeast bench overlooking Salt Lake City. This facility is just one of about twenty-five hospitals world-wide where they graciously assist children plagued with all types of deformities and injuries, at no expense to the kids or their parents. Funding is provided by members of the Shiners Lodge and charitable contributions donated by community and business organizations. Undoubtedly, I was also going to be a recipient of their magnanimous service.

As we drove to the hospital, I was surprised to see how enormous it was. It was as large as a hotel; it was nothing like the hospitals where I had stayed. As we walked through the doors, I noticed the tall ceilings, tile floors, painted walls and the familiar scent of anesthesia that lingers in the halls of every hospital. That smell was almost like a "Welcome Home."

We approached the half-circle service area where a receptionist, overlooking the counter, welcomed us and made small talk with my companion and me. However, I did not understand a single word of English.

After a short period of time, while admission papers were being completed, we were led up the stairs to where I would be staying for a few days: the isolation room. I did not realize I was going to be isolated from the rest of the children for precautionary purposes. I assumed this was going to be my very own room, with my own bathroom, nice bed and a television. After looking over my room, I thought, "This isn't going to be so bad, after all."

After making sure everything had been arranged for me, my escort gave me a hug, then turned me over to the attending nurse. The nurse helped me change into some shorts, a T-shirt and white socks provided by the hospital. I was then immediately escorted into my "room."

CHAPTER 6

Shriners Hospital— Temporary Shelter

*H*ere I was, finally in America! Perhaps not as glamorous as I thought it would be, but nonetheless, on American soil, (well, more like hospital tiled floors.) Sitting there, in my new "suite," I began to be inundated with all types of emotions. Even though I felt secure in my new environment, I think it finally sank in that I was thousands of miles from familiar places and faces. I sat on my bed and began to sob inconsolably.

Upon hearing my cries, a nurse walked in to console me and wipe away my tears. In broken Spanish, she patiently inquired what was the matter. I told her, and somehow she was able to calm my worries and soothe my fears. Instead of preoccupying my mind with anxieties, she suggested I watch a television program. With a remote control she magically turned on the T.V. that was bolted to the wall directly across from the foot of my bed. There before my very eyes, I was drawn to the color monitor.

Wow! I had only heard of *color* television. Without

hesitation, I began pushing the buttons on the remote to find that all of the stations were just a blurb to me. I frantically searched for my favorite shows: Zorro, Rin Tin Tin and Godzilla. But, instead, Gilligan's Island, Charlie's Angel's, Zoom, and Sesame Street panned across the screen. I tolerated Gilligan's Island. I was amused by Charlie's Angel's, and decided to settle for Zoom and Sesame Street because, at least, they had some character skits, and sometimes Big Bird and Grover spoke in Spanish. I must confess that after a while, Gilligan's Island grew on me, even to the point that I found myself screaming out of nowhere, "Skipper!"

Coincidentally, sometime during my stay at Shriners, Bob Denver, the actor who portrayed the character of "Gilligan," paid us a visit. If I recall correctly, he looked as goofy in person as he did on T.V. I was a little disappointed with his visit, however. Although I did appreciate his good will visit, it's just that I would have rather have shaken hands and received a hug from Ginger. Who wouldn't? Oh well, I echo those same words from a famous Rolling Stones song, "You can't always get what you want!"

During the days of my isolation, I was visited by Dr. Andrew Peterson and his beautiful wife, Chris. My first impression of Dr. Peterson was that of a "gringo" Goliath with a giant smile and glistening white teeth. I later learned he was a dentist.

As if his smile wasn't enough to make me feel welcome, they both stretched out their arms and embraced my little body, giving me a feeling of warmth and comfort. To my amazement, Dr. Peterson began talking to me in Spanish, "Bien venido Abelito, mi nombre es Andrew Peterson." (Welcome little Abel, my name is Andrew Peterson.)

After his introduction, he briefly told me about himself, his family and his work. Just the fact that he spoke Spanish was reason enough for Andrew to be my friend for life. I felt an instant bond with Andrew Peterson, knowing that I could communicate with him in my own language. But beyond his linguistic ability, Andrew made me feel like his own son, returning home from a trip to Disneyland.

He literally took upon himself the immense responsibility of being my legal guardian and friend. After our brief interaction, he gave me a hug and told me that he would continue to visit me throughout my stay at Shriners. I took comfort in knowing that he would do just that.

During my three-day isolation, blood was drawn, shots were given, and tests were taken to determine if I was infected with any kind of disease, infection or illness that could be contracted by the other patients. After presenting me with a clean bill of health, I was allowed to bunk with the rest of the children. I was transferred into a familiar scene: the boys' hospital ward.

Picture a long hall with a low wall running down the center. On either side of the center wall were beds lined up next to each other. The only privacy provided was a curtain that could slide between each bed. The beds facing east had a view of the mountains, while the beds facing west had the view of the Salt Lake Valley.

During my stay at Shriners, I was able to experience both scenes. I preferred the view of the valley, especially during the evenings with the whole city lighted up. At the end of the ward was an activities room with desks, a T.V., a chalkboard, and other things to entertain our curiosities.

During the next couple of weeks, to my immense surprise, I discovered that several of my roommates spoke Spanish. That helped me to become comfortable with my new friends and surroundings. As with the rest of the hospitals in which I had spent time, I thought this would be my home for several years.

I slowly became accustomed to the food (which I found hard to swallow at the beginning). On Monday nights, we were served chicken and mashed potatoes. Tuesday nights were hamburger nights. Wednesday nights were spaghetti nights, and so on. We knew what we might expect to be fed on any given day and night. Some meals were better than others. I despised hamburgers, at the beginning. However, the more I hesitantly ate them, the more I became fond of the beefy (I hope it was beef) patty meals. In fact, I looked forward to Tuesdays because it meant only two things, greasy hamburgers and oily fries! Yum, Yum! I guess it could have been more appropriately called, "High Cholesterol Night."

Besides being routinely pricked by needles, exposed to X-ray machines, and being confined to our beds, the hospital was sure to involve us in extra curricular activities. Every day different activities were arranged for us. Sometimes, we were taken outside to play on the lawn and to simply enjoy the warm temperatures. It was also a nice break from being cooped up inside all of the time. The majority of the time we spent playing games in a large room, designed for various recreational activities.

One of my favorite games was wheelchair hockey. Participants, whether wheelchair bound or not, had to be in a wheelchair to play the game. With a hockey stick in hand, we all wheeled around to have a chance to hit the puck. I think the biggest kick we got from the game was bumping into one another's wheelchairs. It didn't take much to amuse us!

This room also was equipped with table games: a pool table, a foosball table, an air hockey table and a ping pong table. I enjoyed playing all of those games, but I seemed to grasp the game of pool best. One may wonder how I was able to hold the stick and hit the balls with only one hand? Well, let me give away my secret. I used my foot! Because of the height of the table, I had to stand on a chair to give me a little height advantage. I then placed my right foot (with a sock) on the table and with the end of the stick in my hand I placed the tip of the stick between my big and second toe. This gave perfect leverage and balance to my game. In fact, my shots were pretty much on cue. Anybody up for a challenge?

A good portion of our time was also occupied by attending some kind of school at the hospital. In the recreational room, desks were set up like a class room—chalkboard and all. Books adorned the shelves along the wall. We were taught the basics: reading, writing and arithmetic.

It was a good thing too, because I didn't know a word of English. At the age of ten, I should have been reading at a fifth-grade level; however, my language barrier hindered that skill. Slowly, but surely, by practicing and constant repetition, mere letters began to spell out words with definite meanings. Soon, I was finding it difficult to retain my primary language, Spanish.

CHAPTER 7

"Hooked"

With all the fun I was having, it was inevitable that surgeries had to be performed on my left hand—that is why I was there in the first place. I cannot count the number of surgeries that were performed on my left hand, including previous operations in Bolivia, but it would be safe to say it is more than I can count on all my existing fingers (five.) I am certain that four of those surgeries were performed at Shriners Hospital.

The severe damage to my hand posed a great challenge to the doctors. I was assigned to a skilled surgeon: Dr. Mark. H. Greene. His preliminary diagnosis of my arm was that from shoulder to elbow, there seemed to be full range of motion and relatively good strength. At that point he noted my having neutral dorsi flexion (backward flexion) of the wrist which was weak in strength.

He concluded that there existed a radial deviation and radial subluxation (a partial dislocation) and some shortening of the radial component. The remaining motor motion of my hand was very limited. He also found that I had some flexion extension of my 4th and 5th fingers, but the remainder of my digits were flaccid (lacked muscle tone). Finally, he determined sensation in my hand and fingers was normal.

In laymen's terms, I had severe bone, tendon, and skin damage and disfigurement. The conclusion was that I could not pick up or even hold objects in a normal manner. So, Dr. Greene, and his team of resident doctors, had the daunting task of performing several reconstructive surgical procedures on my left hand. Of all the surgeries performed, none has been as significant to me as the one which was performed to benefit my index finger.

As I have mentioned, my index finger had no movement of any kind, as a result of the tendon damage. In order to restore motion once again to my index finger, it was necessary to do a tendon graft. The doctors made an incision just above my right ankle and cut a portion of my Achilles tendon, extending to the Plantaris tendon.

They then removed the tendons and inserted them into my thumb and index finger. Now, properly placed and connected to muscles, nerves and tissues, I regained flexibility in my long-dormant finger. That simple procedure to a complex problem made an incredible difference in the way I am able to accomplish things.

Even though my finger does not have great dexterity, I have enough flexibility to perform primary tasks, that I would otherwise not be able to do, prior to my surgery. This realization has given me a greater appreciation for the somewhat limited use of my hand. But more than this understanding, I have determined not to take for granted the privileges, gifts, talents and the little things in life. We are often, too quick to overlook or dismiss the blessings we have right before our eyes.

For most people, holding a pencil, handling a utensil, making a fist, clutching a steering wheel, swinging a tennis racket and buttoning their shirt are things they do subconsciously every day. Not because they are unimportant or less meaningful; they have simply become "second nature" to a person.

For me, these simple functions are an every-day struggle, which I have adapted to my situation to fit my needs. Do we really appreciate what we have physically, materialistically, emotionally, or spiritually, and only notice their absence when they slip from our grasp?

I am frequently approached by individuals who have injured their arms somehow, and have lost the use of their hands. They now find they have something in common with me, and offer comments, such as: "Abel, I now have a better appreciation for the way you handle things with only one hand!" or "I can't believe how much I take for granted the use of my hands!"

After hearing their explanations, I sympathize with them because it is so true! We do tend to take things for granted, without realizing it, especially when it comes to our families. Instead of taking things for granted, may I share a couple of suggestions? First and foremost, thank the good Lord for all that you have. He giveth and He taketh away.

Never leave home without telling your loved ones you love them, even if you have had an argument or disagreement. In the end nothing else matters more than your family. Take the time to spend *quantity* time more than *quality* time with your loved ones. Quality time is usually scheduled, formal, cold, shallow.

Quantity time is more spontaneous, casual, warm, remembered and cherished. Quantity time leads to quality moments. If we develop these habits, our priorities will become focused, preventing us from making the mistake of treating our families like ordinary people. Let us not become victims of familiarity, so that we forget to show our loved ones how much we care for them. Remember, if we plant these kinds of seeds of kindness, we will harvest a wealth of happiness.

Another challenge for the doctors was to fit me with a prosthetic device to substitute for my missing right arm. In most cases, an individual wearing an artificial arm has at least a portion of their existing shoulder or elbow to give them the ability to maneuver the prosthesis. However, in my case, I don't have these extensions or "stumps" as they are called. Since my entire right shoulder was amputated, I am completely flat on my right side. In order for me to have a full, functioning "arm," doctors had to first create a shoulder to which they could connect the prosthetic "arm."

I spent numerous hours, covered in plaster from my neck to my belly, so they could develop a mold from the shape and contour of my upper torso. From the mold, they were able to construct a functionable "arm" with a hook to serve as my hand. The doctors decided that a "hook" would be most appropriate for my needs instead of a hand made out of plastic with no functionality. The "hook" would also give me freedom to do certain things—like crushing glass, snagging paper airplanes mid-flight and ripping holes in the bed sheets.

All humor aside, getting used to my new apparatus was quite a challenge. Because it was made out of heavy material, the "hook" placed extra pounds on me. It was sometimes hot and uncomfortable to wear. And in order to make the prosthetic "arm" bend at the elbow and make the hook open and close, I had to operate it with my left arm.

A wire, directly connected from the hook and forearm, was strapped around my back and looped around my left biceps. By flexing my biceps, the hook would open and shut. By lifting my left arm upward, the hook would raise in the same corresponding manner. When stretching my left arm forward, the same would occur on my right side, etc.

Some people are curious to know why I do not wear this "hook" anymore. I jokingly respond to them that I got rid of my "hook" because every time I would reach to scratch my left eye, a hook would be stabbing me in the right eye! You get the picture! Having already lost a substantial portion of my body on my right side, I was a bit anxious to preserve what remained.

Try as they might, the doctors could not develop an "arm" to meet my needs satisfactorily. Nevertheless, I manage rather well with the use of only one arm, and I am glad that I have learned to maximize the use of the faculties I do enjoy.

CHAPTER 8

P.M.A. (Positive Mental Attitude)

*O*ne of the more poignant lessons I learned during my five months stay at Shriners Hospital was the value of a positive attitude. A young patient from Idaho, by the name of Victor, taught me the importance of what it means to posses a positive attitude, no matter what the circumstances, trials or tribulations. I was only ten-years-old when I was educated about attitude.

At that time, if someone were to ask me to elaborate or draw a diagram about this important subject, I am certain I could not have done it. Even today, I do not profess to know all of the logic behind the positive attitude. However, more importantly, what I did learn from my friend at Shriners, was that we all have the capacity to develop a positive attitude. Let me share what I have come to learn.

On the surface, attitude is the way we communicate our mood to others. When we are optimistic and anticipate successful encounters, we transmit a positive attitude and people usually respond favorably. When we are pessimistic and expect the worst, our attitude is often negative and people tend to avoid us.

Consider the story of the father with twin sons. One was a pessimist, the other an optimist. One day, while the boys were in school, the father decided to surprise his sons with gifts. He filled the pessimist's room with every electronic toy imaginable, feeling satisfied these things would bring much happiness to this boy's life.

The optimist's room he filled with manure. When the boys came home from school, they both went to their separate rooms. The father walked by the pessimist's room and noticed him crying, screaming and throwing a tantrum. The father asks, "What's the matter son, why are you crying?" The boy responded bitterly, "Dad, you didn't get me the right presents! All these toys require a battery; when they run out what am I going to do?"

Saddened by the boy's response, the father walked away, passing by the optimist's room. From the corner of his eyes, he noticed something peculiar. He stopped in his footsteps, turned around, and stood at the door of the optimist's room. He noticed the boy, with a huge grin on his face, diving in and out of the manure. At one point the father asked the optimistic son, "Why are you so happy and why are you jumping through the manure?" The boy happily responded, "Dad, thank you for the manure. I know that wherever there is manure, there's got to be a pony!"

People will react to whatever we transmit through our outward appearance or behavior. It all starts in our head. Attitude is a mind-set. What we think out, we will act out. The "Good Book" teaches us, "As a man thinketh, so is he." In a sense, attitude is how we mentally focus on our outside environments. Like using a video camcorder, for example, we can zoom in and focus the lens on what appeals to us.

We can take any situation in life and transform it into a negative or positive experience. For instance, a rainy day can either be cool, refreshing and beautiful, or gloomy, dark and ugly. Work can be either rewarding or mundane. We may find exercise either energizing or exhausting. However, as we perceive a situation, it is within our power to use it to our advantage, or to be broken by its sharp edges.

To illustrate: Victor was a patient at Shiners Hospital, during the same period I was admitted. He had been treated for a gun-shot wound to his right hand. Reconstructive surgery and skin grafts were performed to mend his joints, skin, and nerves. For the tissue to heal properly, doctors had to make an incision in the outer walls of his abdomen, place his grafted hand inside his abdomen, and sew it in place. By sealing the hand within that organic environment, it was insulated against infection.

This procedure also allowed the hand to be healed by the body's own regenerative powers. I must say that it seemed strange (and a bit surreal) to observe the outline of his thumb against the abdominal wall, as he flashed me the "thumbs-up" sign. Needless to say, I was impressed by this boy's character.

As the great writer Charles Woodson said:

> ". . .*The surest revelation of one's character is the way one bears one's suffering. Circumstances and situations may color life, but by the grace of God, we have been given the power to choose what that color should be. The effect that misfortune, handicap, sickness, and sorrow have upon life is determined by the way in which we meet them.*"

And what, after all, embodies a positive and dynamic

approach to a problem more than the "thumbs-up" sign? What we have to do, symbolically, my friend had to do literally—to reach inside and to not only find, but demonstrate a courage that communicated itself to me in the form of a positive attitude.

One may think or say that it is difficult to be positive in such a negative world. I agree! No one ever said it would be easy, only that it would be worth it. By nature, we are habit-ridden people. We are hesitant to make changes in our lives. We struggle with simply choosing which clothes to wear each morning. But struggle is good! Just like staying concentrated on a diet, or staying on schedule with a project, or keeping focused on a personal goal, all require commitment and a little, or in some cases, a great deal of struggle.

It takes habit-forming, behavioral changes and a lot of patience to elevate ourselves from pessimism to optimism. It is an every day process. A process that will be affected by personal disappointments, health concerns, self-image problems, and media stimuli. Regardless of the outside elements, we can all achieve a positive attitude. We need to be willing to take the first step to make that change. Case in point:

There is a story told of a young man named Adam who got a job at a large chain retail store as an errand boy in the shipping department. Every day it was "Adam, do this." "Adam, do that." "Adam, go here." "Adam, go there." "Adam, bring this to me." "Adam, take that to them." Everybody bossed him around. After several weeks of this treatment, his temper began to escalate. He approached his boss and told him, "I've had it! You can take this job and go jump in a lake!"

Now the boss, rather amused by the young man's behavior, said to Adam, "How would you like to have someone to boss around?" Adam's eyebrows raised, and a little sinister smile crept across his face as he said, "More than anything on earth.

Where is he?" The boss said, "His name is Adam and he is in your department." Adam looked rather puzzled and said, "I'm the only Adam in the shipping department." The boss smiled and said, "I know. See what you can do with his attitude."

Here are a few of my observations about the difference between the negative and positive person:

When climbing a mountain, the negative person looks forward to coming down. A positive person looks toward the top.

When confronted with trials, the negative person falls to his knees and cries "Why me?" The positive person falls to his knees gives thanks for the challenge and asks for strength.

The negative person sees obstacles as barriers. The positive person sees obstacles as opportunities.

On a stormy day, the negative person only sees dreariness and grey. The positive person envisions blue, above a dark and cloudy sky.

A negative person criticizes others for their failures. A positive person encourages others to become their best.

When crossing the finish line, the negative person complains that his hard work made the race barely worth it. The positive person gives credit to hard work for his victory.

The negative person looks back at his life and rarely sees the good, regrets the bad and complains about the future. A positive person looks back at his life and recognizes the good, accepts the bad and looks toward a bright future.

Let me conclude my thoughts on *attitude* by including a phrase by Charles Swindoll, that in my view, sums up my belief about the principle of attitude.

> *"The longer I live, the more I realize the impact of attitude on life. Attitude, to me, is more important than facts. It is more important than the past, than education, than money, than circumstances, than failures, than successes, than what other people think or say or do. It is more important than appearance, giftedness, or skill. It will make or break a company. . .a church. . .a home. The remarkable thing is we have a choice, everyday, regarding the attitude we will embrace for that day. We cannot change our past. . .we cannot change the fact that people will act in a certain way. We cannot change the inevitable. The only thing we can do is play on that one string we have, and that is our attitude. . .I am convinced that life is 10% what happens to me and 90% how I react to it. . .And so it is with you. . .we are in charge of our attitudes."*

CHAPTER 9

"Going Home"

---

*W*e have read and heard of great miracles which have been performed over the centuries: eyesight being restored to the blind; motion and feeling regained to broken limbs of the lame; people being cleansed from the vileness of leprosy; even the dead being brought back to life. The grandness and physical nature of these miracles have a tendency to overshadow the subtler miracles that have taken place, such as being able to withstand evil and overcome temptations; finding peace and comfort in an uncertain world, no matter the consequences, and being able to love and be loved under any conditions.

To be able to recognize these sometimes elusive events in our lives is a miracle in and of itself. I would be a most unworthy beneficiary, were I not to acknowledge the abundant miracles that have transpired throughout my life.

From my humble beginnings in Bolivia, through my life-threatening accident, during my years in hospitals, in the midst of confusions and misunderstandings of growing up, even to this day, the good Lord has never abandoned me.

Caringly and lovingly, He has sent people to care for my needs, to ease my pains, soothe my sorrows, wipe away my tears, calm my worries, and relieve my fears. Each of them has gone to great lengths. Each of them has gone "out on a limb" to help make my life significant and profound. I want to share the story of two such individuals.

Just a couple of days after my admission to Shriners Hospital, while sitting on my bed in my usual hospital attire of a t-shirt, shorts and white socks, Andrew Peterson returned to visit me, just as he said he would. However, I noticed he was not alone. Beside him, stood a handsome couple in their early forties. In his gentle, striking voice, Andrew introduced them to me as Jeron and Annette Davis. He mentioned that he was a cousin to their children and that he was Annette's nephew. He briefly explained that he had described me and my situation to them and that they had felt impressed to visit me at the hospital.

After Andrew finished his introduction, the Davises approached my bed, and as best as they could, they greeted me in Spanish with their "gringo" accent. Our remaining time was spent in light conversation. I did not know what to make of their attention, nor did I completely understand why they were visiting me, although that visit would change the course of my life. How the Davises came to know about me is a miracle in itself!

While attending a Fourth of July rodeo in the beginning weeks of July, 1976, in Oakley, Utah, Annette had broken the filling of one of her lower molars, while biting into an uncooked popcorn kernel. The following morning she telephoned her dentist, Wayne Peterson, who is the father of Andrew Peterson. The receptionist told her that Wayne was out of town but that perhaps Dr. Andrew Peterson could take her in as an emergency patient. As God would have it, Dr. Andrew Peterson was able to treat Annette that very same day.

During Annette's dental procedure, Andrew began casual conversation about Annette's family; "How they were doing?" "What were all of the kids up to?" and so on. He was also interested in knowing how their recently-adopted daughter was doing. Adoption was one of the things they both had in common. Andrew and his wife had recently adopted a baby boy from Bolivia. Of course, their conversation was a one-sided discussion, with Andrew doing all the talking and Annette doing all the listening and nodding. At one point, Andrew began telling Annette my story. He told her of my accident, the hospitals in Bolivia, Luz's efforts, the Shriners Hospital, and his responsibility as my legal guardian. He also explained to her that he was in the process of locating a family to adopt me.

Annette found my story fascinating. So fascinating, in fact, that as she drove home from her appointment, she couldn't get me out of her mind. Being a religious person, a church hymn kept playing *(Thy Spirit Lord Has Touched My Soul)* as an indication that she needed to listen to her heart and to consider the warm feelings she was experiencing. That evening when her husband arrived home from work, she immediately told him about my story, and her overwhelming feeling that they needed to do something for me.

After carefully listening to her explanations, he responded by saying, "We're raising eight kids as it is; one more can't hurt!" Without hesitation, Jeron Davis called Andrew Peterson and informed him that they were very interested in adopting me. Andrew graciously accepted the offer, but also advised them that there was a childless couple interested in me as well. Andrew also mentioned to them the fact that he and his wife were contemplating the possibility of adopting me.

The strongest reason Andrew outlined the other possibilities for my adoption, was that he wanted to make certain that I was going to live with the most ideal family. Therefore, he told Jeron that he was going to thoroughly weigh my options and pray for the right answer. But, in the meantime, he would be happy to take Jeron and Annette to meet me at Shriners Hospital.

Andrew and Jeron scheduled a visit with me the following day: the beginning of new and wonderful relationship.

Shortly after our first couple of visits, Andrew notified the Davises that he had come to the conclusion they were the ideal family for me to join. Meanwhile, I was still oblivious to what was developing between the Davises and myself. As far as I was concerned, Shriners Hospital was my home and the Davises were volunteers, sent to be my mentors on a temporary basis. But I became more puzzled by those assumptions each time the Davises visited me.

To keep the momentum of our relationship going, the Davises made a commitment to visit me two to three times a week. Ironically, with each visit, a divine chemistry of love began to develop between us. They treated me as if I were already one of their own children. A week did not go by in which they failed to manifest their sincere affection for me.

I fondly remember one experience of coming out of the anesthesia after my surgery, only to find them sitting next to my bed, caressing my face and giving me words of comfort.

Speaking of words, in order to break the language barrier between us, the Davises developed a clever system to teach me additional English. They brought with them homemade flash cards with different words written on each one. They would then place them on objects that depicted the words on the cards.

That method helped to me associate the word with the object. After some repetition the pronunciation came easily to me with most words. Soon, I began forming sentences which made my better communication possible with my newly-found friends.

My frequent visits with the Davises over a period of several months led to a special kind of relationship, such as I had seldom known in my young life. On occasion, they also brought with them their own children to visit me. The hospital had a policy that only children over a certain age were allowed to visit patients. Therefore, most of my contacts with the Davis's younger children was waving to them from the outside balcony. Their older children were given permission to come up to the dormitory.

I particularly remember Lisa, who was about sixteen-years-old at that time. On one occasion, she brought with her a group of girls as a service project, to participate in the lives of the children at Shriners Hospital. They played games, read books and showed us a movie. During the movie, Lisa sat next to me, like a big sister, and held my tattered hand through the whole movie. I remember having a sense of comfort and a feeling of security, and thinking in my mind that this is what it must feel like, having a sister or a brother. Four months into my stay at Shriners, the Davises and I had become mutually bonded. Our relationship became increasingly stronger. A day didn't go by without my thinking about them. I missed them when they were unable to visit me. I wanted our special association to be more than just a casual weekly visit. I wanted it to last forever.

Years of family deprivation led me to yearn and pray for the Lord to bless me with a miracle: the miracle of a lasting family relationship. The Lord listened to my supplications and was about to open the heavens and pour out the blessings.

Some time near the end of October, 1976, Jeron and

Annette Davis came for their usual visit. But something was different about them, this time. After our hellos, they excitedly led me to the small activities room adjacent to the boys' dormitory. They had me sit on a chair against the wall. Then, they moved a large blackboard and placed it just in front of me. All the while, I didn't know what to make of their strange behavior. Jeron moved a chair next to me, sat down and placed his arm around my good shoulder. Annette stood next to the blackboard and began writing the names of their children on the board.

The list started with Dad (she pointed to Jeron) then Mom (she pointed to herself) then she continued with Mark, Glen, Kent, Lisa, Brook, Seri, Janna, and Rob. Within this list she left a blank space, purposefully, in between Brook and Seri's name. She tenderly looked into my eyes, turned to the board and wrote "Abel" in the deliberately-blank space.

Suddenly, everything she was doing began to make sense to me. I couldn't believe what was transpiring! Could this be real? No sooner than I had realized what was happening, Annette, while pointing to my name on the board, said, "Abelito, we love you! We want you to be our son. Will you come and live with us?" My emotions were almost out of control. This was the day I had been hoping for, these many years. I was finally going home! This was living proof that God answers prayers!

I don't recall anything else that was expressed between us on that autumn day. It was as if time stood still. I don't think the full meaning of it all registered with me, until the following day when the hospital administrator took me aside to reiterate the fact that the Davises were going to adopt me, and that they were going to be my Mom and Dad for the rest of my life. On hearing her explanation I enthusiastically jumped up and down for joy, screaming at the top of my voice, "I have a family. I have a family!"

It was nearly a month later, November 22, 1976, when I finally left the Shriners Hospital with my new Mom and Dad. My adoption was finalized December 16, 1977.

CHAPTER 10

Mom and Dad

I must say something at this point about the remarkable people I refer to as Mom and Dad, who I so much honor and respect. My father, Jeron E. Davis, was born January 16, 1934 in Salt Lake City, Utah to Edward Bone and Ardella Ottley Davis. He is the third of four children. His parents emphasized honesty, work, respect for other people, religion, education and love, while he was growing up. These are the same traits he applies with his own family. He gained his first employment at the age of fifteen, working at a local ice cream shop from 1949 to 1953.

While attending South High School in Salt Lake City, he played drums in the marching band, concert, and pep bands. Besides his instrumental talents, my dad excelled in his speech and science classes. He graduated from his alma mater in 1952. Shortly thereafter, he began his college courses at the University of Utah. His education was abruptly interrupted when Uncle Sam called. He was drafted into the United States Army in 1954.

Upon his honorable discharge in 1956, he continued his education, ultimately graduating with a Bachelor of Science Degree, with a major in business, in 1961. He worked for a couple of companies as a salesman, until he started his own specialty advertising business in 1969. His hard work and dedicated service have led him to a successful career.

My mother, Ruth Annette Parker Davis, was born January 29, 1934 in Salt Lake City, Utah to Casper Hugh and Carrie Hansen Parker. She is the youngest of four children. Her parents stressed honesty, integrity, dependability, religion, and family unity. She has encouraged her children to honor those same values in her own home. While attending East High School in Salt Lake City, she enjoyed Home Economics, where she furthered her cooking, sewing and home management talents. She was also a member of concert choir and the ski club. She graduated from her alma mater in 1952. I consider my mother a real "people" person. She cherishes the friends she has made since her high school days, and she loves the times she spends with them. But the main priority in her life has been her children and her thirty-four grandchildren (and counting).

I am including here, my mother's own account how she met my father. I love this story, and feel it is more appropriate that she tell it in her own words. I retrieved this article she wrote from our family's bimonthly newsletter:

As a young teenager, my girlfriends and I used to have lively discussions on how we might meet our future husbands. . . .would it be at college or did we already know him? . . . would he be in one of our classes? . . . would a friend line us up? . . . would he be handsome? . . . what would our first date be like? . . . etc. I never dreamed I would meet the man I would marry through one of my own family members.

The year was 1951 and I was 17-years-old. It was the end

of May or beginning of June that my sister, Marilyn, told me about this cute boy that was working for them at their Fernwood Ice Cream and Candy store. His name was Jerry Davis. "Oh, Annie," she said, "we have got to introduce you. He is such a cute boy and really on the ball." I thought it sounded like a great idea and he agreed to it, also.

The plans were laid. My sister Virginia, and family were up from Mt. Pleasant, Utah and we were all going to the zoo. On the way home, we would stop in at Fernwood's for a treat. Jerry would be working that day and would wait on us. He would recognize who I was because he had been told I would be wearing a lavender dress with a purple flower on it.

On the day scheduled, I was somewhat nervous but it was worse for Jerry. The rest of the employees knew what was going on and everyone was waiting for us to come in. Jerry was in the back doing the dishes when Marie, one of the employees yelled, "Here she comes." Jerry's hands immediately began to shake and it didn't get any easier because the plan was for him to wait on our table. To make matters worse, his boss, who is my brother-in-law, was with us. It was really quite a miserable experience for Jerry.

As I remember, we were introduced and then we all gave our ice cream orders. I thought he was more than cute. . .he was handsome. I knew I would like to go out with him but had no clue as to whether he would call me or not. The ball was in his court and I would just have to wait and see. A week went by. . .no call. I decided maybe it would be a good idea if I went in for an ice cream cone.

Luckily, no other customers were there but that did not last long. Jerry waited on me and as I sat up to the counter and we began to talk, who should walk in but his father. It was only a few minutes later that a large group came in and that was the *end of our conversation. I left soon after that. As I drove off, I thought to myself, "Well, that's the end of that. I'll never hear from him." Nevertheless, I hoped he would call.*

Another week went by and every time the telephone rang, my heart would jump in hopes that it was him. Finally, at the end of the week, the long awaited call came.

I couldn't believe it when my Mother told me that I was wanted on the phone and that it was a "boy" calling. Those kind of phone calls were few and far between. I was not popular in high school and my dating record was nothing to brag about. You can imagine how my heart was pounding when I said, "Hello" and heard a male voice answer, "Hi, this is Jerry Davis."

Our first date was quite an experience. Jerry had purchased a new motorcycle several months earlier and it was his pride and joy. He asked me to go on a motorcycle ride. I am surprised my Mother let me go. I wouldn't be too happy about my daughter going off on a motorcycle ride. . .especially with a boy we didn't know.

Finally, the day for our date arrived. I was both excited and nervous. When we got out to the curb and were ready to get on the motorcycle, I noticed that the seat really wasn't designed for two people to sit on it. No matter. . .I was skinny then so I just scooted up close to Jerry and since I didn't want to fall off, I wrapped my arms around him.

We probably spent two hours riding through the neighborhoods along Foothill Drive and Wasatch Boulevard. As we were coming down 21st South, Jerry mentioned once or twice that I was dragging my feet. I wasn't aware of it and thought that was strange. When we arrived back at my home, Jerry got off the motorcycle and waited for me to do likewise.

I went to climb off, only to find that I had no feeling in my legs and was unable to stand up, let alone throw my leg over to climb off. The end result was that Jerry had to drag me off of the motorcycle, across the sidewalk and set me down on the grass. Talk about making a good first impression.

The only thing that we could figure out was that since the seat really was meant to hold just one person, my being there caused Jerry to partially sit on my legs; thus, the circulation was cut off and my legs went numb. This was the reason for dragging my feet.

As the saying goes, "All's well that ends well." Jerry asked me for another date. To be on the safe side though, we went to a movie.

This year will mark my parents' forty-fourth anniversary. Theirs is a relationship I admire. They both take their roles as parents seriously. Mom took pride in being a homemaker. She ran a well-kept, well-organized home. As difficult as it might have been sometimes, her faith never wavered in rearing eleven children. Her most cherished moments were spending time with her family.

Whether it was washing dishes right beside her children, driving them to various activities, reading the scriptures, disciplining moments, or family vacations, Mom loved to be with us. Even today, with all of her children out on their own, she looks forward to Sunday visits, birthdays, anniversaries, church activities and any excuse to be with her children and grandchildren.

Dad is a responsible father. His role as the sole provider for the family was played exceptionally well. He was disciplined and committed to making ends meet for our large family. I am certain my parents experienced hard times, but we never knew it. We always had food to eat and clothes to wear. Even though Dad worked hard, he never sacrificed his time with his family. We were his priority. There were hikes in the mountains, picnics in the park and vacations to Zion's, Grand Canyon, Mount Rushmore National Parks, Capistrano Beach, California, Tijuana, Mexico and much, much more.

Dad was always a fountain of advice. He would caution us, "If you're coasting, you're going down hill." Other famous quotes from dad: "A chicken doesn't stop scratching just because the worms are scarce." and "Do it right the first time!"

Sometimes, we would have to ponder the meaning of his advice, but nevertheless, we felt we were guided by a wise man. I would take his sound counsel over any one else's. My father has a tender side to him. This trait would often be apparent the way he revered his wife. He was never shy in showing his love for her in front of us children. The lingering kisses, the constant hugs, the romantic hand holding and the occasional pat on the derriere, exemplified a couple well in their forties, still madly in love. He continues this same adoration, today.

I want to share a story my father wrote in one of our family newsletters. It will suggest how he learned to be a family man from his father. My dad writes about a comical hunting episode with his father.

∽

Time For Deer Hunting
or
Time Turned On It's Head

"Let's go to bed early so we can get up plenty early. We'll want to go up the mountain while it's still dark." I nodded my approval, knowing that Dad always liked to start out early when we went hunting. The camp fire could wait until tomorrow.

We had driven through Coalville and then East into the mountains of the Chalk Creek Valley. Dad and I were always ready for a good deer hunt and were happy as we pulled into a good camp spot at the base of some likely-looking mountains for our special permit hunt. The prospects were for warm sleeping because Dad had converted the back of his 1937 Ford for sleeping. We could lie with our feet in the trunk and our bodies in the back seat area. That gave us a soft bed and, with the rear windows, we had some control over the cold mountain air as we slept.

We needed a place to cook and eat, so we set up our umbrella tent. With our gas stove, Dad cooked a tasty supper. Though the food was basic, our appetites were stimulated by the mountain air and the prospects of tomorrow's hunt.

The white full moon hung over the cold November mountains to the East, as we got into the car and anxiously got ready for a good sleep, so we'd be ready in the morning. I loved the hunt, even though I was only 14-years-old and couldn't yet carry a gun. Dad said, "We ought to get up at five o'clock, so that we can have time to cook breakfast before we head out. Let's not over-sleep."

I took my watch off my wrist and set it in a safe place where I could get it in the dark of the night. We chatted for a bit about how we would hunt the mountain in the morning. Then we turned over and went to sleep.

I woke up with a start. "Hope we haven't overslept." My watch was easy to find in the dark. With the moon shining through the side window, it wasn't hard to see that it was time to get up. "Dad, it's five minutes to five. It's time!" Anxious to not be late for the hunt, Dad hurried to get his watch. He checked it with his flashlight and said, "Sure enough, time to get up." We quickly got dressed and went into the cooking tent to prepare breakfast.

What a wonderful breakfast! Even though we were not very hungry because of the exciting prospects of hunting, we had bacon & eggs and pancakes with all the trimmings. That was topped off with a couple of cups of hot chocolate. Then we prepared for the hunt: we put on our hunting jackets with the huge pockets which could hold our day's supplies. . .water, sack lunches, apples, candy, toilet paper, ammo, dragging rope, sharp knife. . .we were ready! Time for us to get Dad's 300 Savage from the car and load up.

When we stepped out of the tent, we felt that there was something wrong. There was no light of daybreak in the Eastern sky. Even with the full moon overhead, the morning was still dark. I said, "The moon hasn't moved much since last night, has it." Dad took a long skyward look. He had a quizzical look on his face as he struggled to pull out his pocket watch. Peering down, he tried to get a good look at it in the dark. Then he pulled his flashlight from his pocket, trying again to read his watch. "My gosh, Jerry! It's only 12:10!" We couldn't believe it! How could we have gotten up so early? We stood in disbelief, just looking at one another.

"What time was it when you woke me up?" "4:55. What did your watch say?" "Almost five o'clock." He mused. "Is it possible that you had your watch turned up-side-down?" "I

don't know. Maybe. Why?" "If your watch was up-side-down, and it read 4:55. . .if it were right-side-up, it would read 11:25. Jerry, we got up at 11:25! No wonder the moon hasn't moved much!"

We were stunned! How could I have made such a mistake? How could Dad have double checked the time and read his watch the same way? No wonder we weren't hungry as we ate. We talked about what to do now and concluded that we should go back to bed. It was as though we were living life a second time.

At five o'clock, we got up again, ate another breakfast, and started trudging up the dark mountain to begin the hunt.

∽

It is not difficult for one to see why I respect and honor my parents to such a great degree. They have educated me in the ways I should conduct my life. They have taught me principles by which to live by. They are an example to me of what a parent should be like. They are my heroes. They make it justifiably simple to revere them as Mom and Dad.

CHAPTER 11

Sibling Hierarchy

I have three sisters and seven brothers. They are all unique and individually packaged. A common thread that binds us all together is our religion. We are all members of The Church of Jesus Christ of Latter-day Saints (LDS) more commonly known as "Mormons." Our beliefs, principles, and values are based upon the teachings of the gospel of Jesus Christ. That gospel has been the focus of life for our entire family.

My eldest brother, Mark, lives in the small town of Oakley, Utah, about forty-five miles east of Salt Lake City. He favors the country atmosphere, versus the hustle and bustle of the city. He seems more reserved and quiet than the rest of my siblings. When he was nineteen-years-old, (the age when LDS young men are encouraged to serve a full-time proselyting mission) he was called to serve a mission for the Church. He served two years in Houston, Texas, preaching the gospel like Paul of Damascus, in the New Testament.

He is a proud father of seven children. His beautiful wife,

Jane, keeps a clean and well-organized home. Jane also home-schools four of their seven children. Mark and Jane believe this non-traditional method of education has been both a positive and rewarding experience for their entire family. Mark operates his own business as a master electrician. Mark has never appeared to be extravagant or flashy. He has always chosen to live a simple, yet comfortable life. I have admired that characteristic in Mark. Mark is a respecter of God and a fervent believer in family unity.

The second child is Glen. Glen and his wonderful wife, Janene, are the parents of seven children. They live in Holladay, a suburb south of Salt Lake City. Glen also served a two-year LDS mission in Calgary, Canada. Glen, a graduate of University of Utah, along with his business partner, Kent, my third oldest brother, has followed in the footsteps of my father in owning his own specialty advertising company. Glen is a natural-born salesman. His ability to communicate with people has proven to be an asset throughout his life, not only in his business associations, but with people from all walks of life. It is no wonder that, besides my father, most of my brothers and sisters seek counsel from him with their concerns. On numerous occasions, Glen has given me a listening ear and a helping hand.

Kent, his marvelous wife, Erin, and their five children, live in close proximity to Holladay, a suburb of Salt Lake City. Kent also dedicated two years of his life to a LDS Church mission in Anaheim, California, an experience he attests made him a better man. As I previously mentioned, he, along with Glen, is a joint partner in a specialty advertising business. Kent is a graduate of the University of Utah in business. Besides his family, he is actively involved with his church duties.

My sister, Lisa, whom I have come to call, Lu Lu, is

married to Clyde Campbell, an outstanding brother-in-law. They also live in Holladay with their six children. Lisa has made the wise, but sometimes difficult decision, to stay at home with her children. Lisa has a talent for cutting hair, which she has made into a side business. She too is an active participant in the Church.

Brook, only a few years older than I, lives with his remarkable wife, Michal, and their four children in Olympus Cove, a suburb east of Salt Lake City. Just as his older brothers, Brook, served an LDS mission for two years in Bahia Blanca, Argentina. He still cultivates his ability to speak the Spanish language. A graduate of University of Utah, Brook has also followed in our father's footsteps in owning his specialty advertising business. Brook is a most genuine person. He is honest, sincere and very caring. He demonstrates these sentiments effectively to his family and to his friends.

Joel is the brother I never knew. Prior to my being adopted, Joel passed away. Just six-weeks-old, Joel, quietly, was taken from this earth. The doctors never determined the exact cause of his death. They suggested that viral pneumonia or sudden infant death syndrome may have been the cause. My memory of Joel consists of just a black and white photo, hanging on the family room wall of my parents' home. It is my hope that, some day, after this life, I will have the opportunity to put my arms around my brother, Joel.

Brett is my brother, two years younger than I am. Brett was adopted by my parents from Seoul, Korea when he was eight-years-old. He was abandoned by his biological parents when he was a very young boy. Interestingly enough, Brett's adoption papers were completed prior to mine. However, I was able to come to live with my parents before Brett. I can clearly recall the first time I saw Brett. I had just gotten out of the shower and, to my surprise, there he was, standing on the bathroom sink counter. I thought to myself, "So this is my little brother, Brett."

I noticed his long, straight, black hair, drooping over his dark brown eyes. His round face accented his expansive smile. His scrawny body was covered with scabies, a kind of skin rash he had contracted in Korea. Even though my Dad was dabbing his skin with cotton balls soaked with alcohol, he still managed to demonstrate a cheerful demeanor. In fact, he seemed to be in such a cheerful mood that, upon noticing that I had no right arm, he began to laugh. Upon realizing this, my Dad mentioned to him briefly about my accident, and immediately, Brett stretched out his arms to me and demonstrated brotherly love. That was the beginning of our blossoming friendship.

I am sad to say Brett is no longer with us. During my time, serving an LDS mission, I received word that he had died. I was heart-broken. My father broke the news to me in a telephone call, and explained how he died. Brett had taken his own precious life at the tender age of seventeen. It is not important to relate here the details of his death. Rather, it is more fitting to mention the memories I have of him.

But before I proceed any further, I want to make clear I do not agree with what he did because of the hurt he left behind. The events that led to his ultimate demise, remain inexplicable. However, I want to make it clear that, after much prayer and consideration, the entire family has had a reassurance that Brett is in the arms of our kind, loving and forgiving Heavenly Father.

Brett possessed a lot of great qualities. He was a kind boy. I cannot ever remember him raising his voice to my parents or brothers and sisters. He did not let his temper get the best of him. If we were involved in any confrontations, he would always be the peacemaker. He was gentle and quiet. He was never loud or boisterous. He was remarkable in his understanding of scriptural passages. I believe all those years of getting up early in the morning for scripture study with the family paid off for Brett.

Scholastically, Brett was outstanding. I was always envious of how smart he was. In fact, as a sophomore in high school, Brett was taking some more advanced classes than I was, as a senior. He would often help me with my math homework. I can still picture him at the kitchen table with his nose buried in his school books.

Brett's interests were quite focused, particularly on things relating to good quality electronics. He especially loved stereo systems. Mom and Dad came home one day with a brand new stereo system and Brett was in heaven! He and I would play music, as loud as we could, every chance we got, especially when Mom and Dad were away. I also remember Brett saving up the money he earned from his paper route to buy a Sony Walkman (a hand held stereo). It was his pride and joy.

The last time I saw Brett was at the airport the day of my departure for my mission to the Dominican Republic. We gave each other a tight hug and I expressed my love for him and in turn he expressed his love to me saying, "I love you, big brother." Brett was not only my brother he was my soul mate. I will ever be grateful to my Heavenly Father for giving me the opportunity to have shared part of my life with one of His spiritual giants.

Seri, four years younger than I, lives in Salt Lake City. She was adopted by my parents when she was six-years-old. Working with an adoption agency, my parents adopted Seri from an orphanage in Seoul, Korea. She, too, was abandoned by her natural parents at a tender age. Because of malnutrition,

Seri had complications with her legs. Her feet had a tendency to veer outwards, making it difficult for her to walk correctly.

To remedy the problem, she had to wear leg and foot braces. Eventually, her feet were adjusted to a normal stance. Another condition Seri was plagued with was that both of her eardrums were damaged. Operations were performed to replace them. Seri has always been a hard worker. A great quality of Seri is that she takes pride in her hard work.

Janna, my baby sister, lives with her exceptional husband, David Voss, in East Lansing, Michigan. David is attending medical school at the University of Michigan. Janna has been blessed with many talents, which she has exercised to the best of her abilities. From grade one to her Master's degree in Speech Pathology, Janna has achieved a 3.5 and higher grade point average.

Her other talents include having an exceptional voice for singing, a keen ear for playing the piano, and skilled hands to play the violin. In addition to that, Janna is a remarkable mother to her brand-new baby daughter, Ruth. Because she feels that her family is the top priority in her life, it was not a difficult choice for her to quit her job and become a full-time mother.

Last, but not least, is Rob. Married for two years to his beautiful wife Debbie, Rob is still a newlywed. Rob graduated from the University of Utah in the spring of 1997. He plans to launch his own business. In what area? Specialty Advertising, of course. Rob has always been an entrepreneur. In his teens, he ran his own lawn aerating business to earn money for school tuition. At nineteen, he served an LDS mission for two years in Independence, Missouri. Rob is a jack of all trades. In his spare time, he enjoys fixing and making things.

That is my family in a nutshell. There is nothing out of the ordinary about us. Just extraordinary parents who made it their commitment to raise their children in a loving and disciplined home. Our home was governed by rules, and more rules. Chores and school work had to be completed before any kind of play. If we were to be gone on a school night, we needed to return no later than 8:00 and be in bed by 8:30. On weekend nights, curfew was enforced. The latest we were ever allowed to stay out was 12:00 a.m., even into my late teens. Rather than waiting up for us, it was expected that we would report to Mom and Dad after our night out. In the event we neglected to obey this rule, we found ourselves locked out of the house, causing us to have a sleepless night in our car.

Any kind of foul or profane language was not tolerated in our family. In our home outrageous attire, unnecessary accessories (i.e., earrings for the boys, heavy makeup for the girls,) and bizarre hairdos were forbidden. Our television watching was closely monitored. We were limited to certain programs and designated times. We watched only G-rated and PG movies.

Only wholesome and uplifting music was encouraged in our home. Dating was allowed, but serious relationships before our missions were strongly discouraged. To help us avoid serious relationships, we could not date the same girl or boy, consecutively, hopefully, preventing significant relationships. In addition to these rules, we were expected to go to church, obey our leaders, and respect our elders.

One may be surprised at the stringent rules under which we lived. How were our parents able to enforce all these rules with eleven children? On a weekly basis, we held a family council. Monday night was designated as "Family Night." Lessons were given, rules were explained, complaints were resolved, games were played and refreshments were served.

This was a perfect system for my parents to teach us the fundamentals and the purpose of life. Never did my parents teach us a principle or implement a rule by being hypocritical. They were the first ones to walk the walk. Rules were not a means to restrict our individual potential, but were designed to encourage responsibility, accountability and self respect. Were these rules difficult to obey? Of course! I was not the only one of my siblings who, sometimes, resented the restrictions and limitations imposed by the "rules." But did they have a positive affect in our lives? No question about it! Let me relate an example.

It was my graduation night from high school. With the euphoria of graduation and the prospects of freedom from those restrictive family rules, luring me away, I had decided to leave home. I made the decision to move out and be on my own, so that I would no longer have to endure another day under my parents' dictatorial power. I was finally going to enjoy some freedom! Be free to do whatever I wanted to do! No one to tell me what to do! I was certain I was making the right choice.

After I gathered up enough courage, I told my parents sharply, " Mom, Dad, I'm moving to California! I'm going to live in Los Angeles! I'm leaving tomorrow!"

Hearing my rude remarks, my parents were heartbroken. They counseled me against it. They encouraged me not to do it. But in the end, they couldn't stop me from going forward with my plan. Hesitantly, they helped me with the travel arrangements and purchased a one-way bus ticket to L.A. for me. They provided some extra cash to assist me once I arrived at my destination.

The next morning, with my small suitcase in hand, I took one last look around the room I shared with my four older brothers. Deep down inside, I knew was making a big mistake.

How could I possibly leave behind such a solid, principle-based foundation, a family-oriented, value-driven environment to gratify my own selfish desires?

But I was determined to prove to my parents that I did not need their tough love. I was going to make it on my own.

We got in the van and, somberly, drove to the bus station. Once inside the bus depot, I presented my pass to the cashier; then made my way to the departing bus. At the base of the entrance, my parents, individually, took a turn to hug and kiss me for the last time. Separating from my parents was harder than I realized it was going to be.

I held back the tears, as long as I could. After telling them goodbye, I quickly climbed aboard to find my seat. I looked out my window, only to see my parents walking away, with my dad's arm around my mom's shoulder.

Everything that I was feeling, everything that I was holding in, finally, reached the surface. I burst out crying. This was not the way it was supposed to be! This was not the way I was supposed to feel! I was supposed to be happy, rollicking with laughter! This was the freedom I was seeking! What had gone wrong? Who knew it was going end this way? My parents did! I was too caught up in my own little world, unable to see the big picture.

The long drive to Los Angeles provided plenty of time for me to collect my thoughts and do a lot of soul searching, ponder my decision and reflect upon my desires.

It didn't take me long to come to my senses; to stop searching for something that did not exist—freedom without accountability. I knew what I had to do when I arrived in Los Angeles.

Sunday evening, I immediately telephoned home to tell my parents that I had made a terrible mistake. My father answered the telephone. It was so good to hear his voice! I asked him if they would accept me back into their home. He graciously said that they would. I realized that they had known all the time that I would change my mind. But they wanted me to experience for myself the effects of freedom without responsibility. The moment I hung up the phone, I set out to purchase a one-way airline ticket to Salt Lake City. . .and *home!*

A couple of months after my abortive escapade, my father sat me down to tell me what my parents had gone through, during my absence. Even though they knew, deep down inside, that I would return, they wondered how they had gone wrong with me. Had they been too harsh. . .too soft. . .maybe the rules were not clear enough. . .why would I want to leave a home filled with love?

Needless to say, my actions triggered a deep concern in my parents. My mother went into a state of anxiety. I had caused a lot of significant hurt, meaningless pain and inexplicable anguish. My dad's words pierced my heart with great remorse. How could I have overlooked my parents' beneficial intentions? Was I just going through a stage of rebellion, or was this a phase I needed to experience? Whatever the truth may be, I cannot deny the fact that I was derelict in my role as a well-trained son.

Since that dark day, my parents have forgiven me and I have strived to be a more obedient son. In fact, I respect my loving parents to such a great degree, that my wife and I have decided to implement some of the same rules with our own children. God bless the day I met my parents!

CHAPTER 12

I Believe in Me

---

*I*f there is one thing that I would say to summarize all my years with my wonderful parents, it is: "Thank you for nothing." That's right, nothing at all. You see, of their eleven children, I am the only one with a physical disability. I now know that in order for me to become self-reliant, independent, self-assured, and to believe in myself, they had to do what every loving parent should do: nothing! Their belief was that they were not going to treat me any differently, or give me special privileges that were not given to the rest of my brothers and sisters.

They didn't totally abandon me, however. They stood back, observed and encouraged me, leaving me to my own devices to do things. For instance, I had to learn how to dress myself, buttoning shirts with my mouth, leaning against a wall to hold my trousers up, so I could buckle my belt.

In order to do the chores around the house, I had to learn how to hold a broom to sweep floors and driveways, maneuver a vacuum to be able to push it back and forth on the carpets, skillfully hold wet dishes and glasses to carefully load them in the dishwasher, tactically handle a push mower to cut the lawns, and to do other tasks.

No matter that most of these things had been done, for the most part, by someone other than myself, for the past seven years, while I had been in a patient in hospitals.

So, in my frustrations, I thought at times, their method of teaching me self-reliance was somewhat distant. Why couldn't they just button my shirt or cut my meat at the dinner table? Or, for that matter, why did they insist I become a newspaper boy, when they knew very well it was going to be a challenge for me to fold the papers with one hand, put a rubber band around them, pick them up, and place them in the bag hanging on the bike handles; only to have them fall out of my arm, so I must start the process all over again.

Not only that, I had to ride my bicycle, balance the extra weight, and deliver the papers to fifty-five customers! Perhaps, I may sound a bit bitter. Nonetheless, it was difficult to successfully fulfill my parents' high expectations. I realize today, that my parents, purposefully, ignited the flame necessary for me to catch the fire that needed to burn within me: the power of believing in myself.

But what does it mean to believe in one's self? It is an inward power, often spoken of, but seldom manifested. On the surface, it empowers what we are capable of becoming. Believing in one's self goes beyond just thinking of what you can do. To truly believe in yourself, you must go through an acceptance process. Sometimes, this is accomplished voluntarily. Other times it is forced upon us. My parents, by forcing me to discover what I could do, ultimately led me to the knowledge and acceptance of who I am, what I am, and the way that I am.

Who am I? From a purely physical standpoint, my body structure is made up of cells, tissue, plasma, bones, skin and so forth. But beyond these substances, we are blessed with hidden capabilities, talents, and powers endowed by the ultimate entity. My personal believe is that I was created by God. Having this belief, as a foundation in my life, gives me comfort and builds confidence in myself.

In one's own discovery, you can reach your own conclusion as to who your maker is. Once we realize this important aspect, we can develop a sense of importance and uniqueness, with great individual potential.

What am I? Just as an engine, transmission, radiator or oil filter are intrinsic parts in a functioning automobile, we each have significant roles we need to fulfill in this life, whether it be small or on a grand scale. It is not critical that we achieve high status or gain financial wealth in this life. More importantly, it is crucial to our stability in life, that we make the most of ourselves, at whatever strata we may find ourselves. Each of us is unique, as a butcher, baker, or candlestick maker. It doesn't matter. Never underestimate your individual worth. The price you place on *yourself* determines the true value of your character.

The way I am? The wonderful thing about the human race is that we all come in different shapes and sizes with distinct principles, values and morals. Over the years, medical technology has given us strategies to alter our physical appearances.

Personal trainers and plastic surgeons are becoming the newly-rich among us. Depending on our personal convictions, we have also made progress in regards to behavioral pattern changes. And yet, many of us are still unsatisfied with our selves, physically, mentally and spiritually.

The missing ingredient: accepting ourselves the way we are. For the rest of my life, I will live with only one arm. This is the way I am going to be! I cannot change that fact! Rather than feeling sorry for myself, crying, "Woe is me! or "Why me?" I have chosen to accept my present situation, exactly the way it is.

That is not to say that I am entirely comfortable with the way I have to do things with just one arm. Who does not depend upon all their body parts? I am just like anyone else in that respect. I would give nearly anything to have my right arm back again. But that is not the point. Whether we are struggling physically, emotionally or mentally, we need to take that all-important step of evaluating our life from the inside out. Discovering happiness and contentment in life evolves from inward transformations, not from outer modifications. We need to be able to look in the mirror, accept the image before us, and say, "That is the *real* me!" I like what Dr. Seuss says about each of us in this classic children's poem:

> *Today you are you! That is truer than true!*
> *There is no one alive that is youer than you!*
> *Shout aloud, "I'm glad to be what I am!"*
> *Thank goodness I am not a clam or a ham*
> *or a dusty old jar of gooseberry jam!*
> *I am what I am! What a great thing to be!*
> *If I say so myself! Happy every day to me!*

Discovering ourselves is the greatest challenge, yet the most rewarding and gratifying task of our lives. Once we have navigated the discovery process of accepting who we are, what we are and the way we are, then, we can begin believing in ourselves. We can then inspire that same confidence in others:

> *If just one person believes in you, deep enough*
> *and strong enough believes in you; Hard*

*enough and long enough, before you knew it,
someone else would think, "If he can do it, I
can do it." Making it two whole people who
believe in you, deep enough and strong enough,
believe in you. Hard enough and long enough
there's bound to be some other person who
believes in making it a threesome, making it
three. People, you can say, believe in me. And
if three whole people, why not four, and if four
whole people, why not more and more and
more. . .And when all those people believe in
you, deep enough and strong enough, and long
enough, it stands to reason, you yourself will
start to see what other people see in you. And
maybe even you can believe in you, too!*

—The Muppets

That belief by others and myself has established a standard
by which I conduct myself in whatever situation I find myself.
In high school, I was on the soccer, football, and diving teams.
I tried out for the swimming team, but after discovering I kept
swimming in circles, the coach encouraged me to try diving,
instead. I had a knack for jumping and doing flips, but there
was no form, finesse and timing to my style.

After a lot of coaching and training, I was able to compete
in two state championship meets. My first year in tournament
competition, I acquired my letterman's jacket. I look at this
achievement and many others as a testament that it is more
productive in life to believe in one's self, than to deny the
realization of your potential.

CHAPTER 13

Love and Laughter

As I mentioned earlier, when I was nineteen-years-old in the summer of 1985, I committed myself to serve a proselyting mission for my church. Two years of sharing a doctrine I believe to be true and serving others proved to be a rewarding and challenging experience. At the conclusion of my mission, I wrote the following:

Here I sit with pen in hand, reflecting over the past two years, sifting through the many memories of my mission. As I'm trying to choose one "special" experience to write about, I'm coming to the conclusion it is futile. There is no "one, single" experience I can choose. For my whole mission was one precious, special experience. An experience that brought depth to my character, vision to my eyes, strength to my testimony and a taste of pure love into my heart.

Like many others, my mission actually began long before my call came, however, that is another chapter. It is sufficient, now, to say it was through a long series of events, controlled by a loving hand of our Heavenly Father that brought me to the point of accepting a call to serve. Nevertheless, at the age of nineteen, I was like any other nineteen-year-old, still playing the games of a teenager. Trying to survive the pains of growing up. Finding it difficult, to say the least, to make the commitment to be a full-time missionary.

One day, however, I quit resisting the prompting and while my folks were away on vacation, I made the necessary preparations and had my missionary papers to the Church headquarters. I received my call in less than a week and found to my surprise that I was to serve in the Santo Domingo, Dominican Republic (a Caribbean island shared with Haiti) Mission.

Sunday, the day after I received my call, my mother, still recovering from the shock, told me that a Church brother within our neighborhood boundaries wanted to talk to me about my mission call. That same evening, I went over to the chapel where I thought I would find this good brother. When I got there, Brother Swensen met me in his office and said, "Brother Davis, come on in. I just thought I would share with you something about your mission call."

I didn't know he was on the General Missionary Committee (the council that arranges missionary calls to prospective missionaries) of the Church. After he told me his position and the role he played in my mission call, he had my undivided attention. He continued, saying, "It was a very interesting and spiritual experience. We were sitting in the Salt Lake LDS Temple, reviewing the calls of the missionaries for that week and we came to your papers.

We read them and found that you had expressed your desire to go to Bolivia to help your own people and, perhaps, to locate your natural parents. We thought that to be a reasonable desire, and were considering, very seriously, sending you to Bolivia.

However, we felt impressed this was not the appropriate time to send you to Bolivia. Brother Dallin H. Oaks, in particular, a member of the missionary council, felt very strongly that you needed to serve the people in the Dominican Republic. He said, "I don't know why, but God knows why, and Brother Davis will know why by the time he returns home." I left the chapel very humbled with a new outlook on my mission call.

The weeks flew by, and before I knew it, I found myself standing in the middle of a whole new world: the Missionary Training Center in Provo, Utah. I honestly thought I would never survive the strict schedules, a twenty-four hour missionary companion, the twelve to fifteen hours a day of studying and learning. This wasn't at all what I thought it would be like. At long last, I finally adjusted to this different way of life when, suddenly, I was thrust into a world I had only learned about in culture class and read about in our reading materials.

I went from clean, white, starched sheets on bunk beds to mosquito nets and foam pads on the floor; from chicken fried steak to rice and beans; wide, carpeted, clean walkways to narrow dirt roads filled with garbage; from a world of white shirts and ties to naked little kids and dirty dirt floors; from long, hot showers to cold bucket baths.

I think this was a part of mission life that my culture class had not prepared me for. Only one week into my service in the small town of San Juan, Dominican Republic, I decided that mission life was not for me. I told my companion I wanted to go home, so we packed my bags and headed for the mission office in Santo Domingo, hoping they still had my return airline ticket.

After some counseling by a loving mission president, continuous prayers on my part and advice from my parents, I mustered enough strength to give it another try. The words of Brother Oaks were just distant, misty words. But, obviously, *someone else clearly recalled his words. For the adversary was working overtime. I had barely become halfway comfortable with this strange way of life, when one bleak afternoon, I received word that my seventeen-year-old brother, Brett, the one I was so close to, had taken his own life.*

I was heartbroken and devastated. I wanted to pack my bags, again, and head back home.

Again, I needed encouragement. I needed some assurance that I was doing the right thing. My mission president instructed me that these were simply obstacles in my way, preventing me from doing the work of the Lord. I needed to surmount them; my place at this time was in the mission field. My family would be blessed. I needed to remember the words of Elder Oaks. By placing trust in God and just putting my shoulder to the wheel and doing the work, the peace, once again, would return to my heart. Step by step, I came to realize that I did have a purpose here.

One of the first experiences that helped me begin to recognize this purpose was in the area of Independencia, Dominican Republic. It was nearing the end of a long, hard, hot, unsuccessful morning. We had been turned away so many times, laughed at, jeered at. . .and it had just been "one of those days." We were discouraged and didn't know where to go, so we prayed for guidance.

Soon, we found ourselves in an area we had never visited before. We began following our hearts and walked up a narrow trail between small, wooden shacks. We kept going, until we came to a man who was holding a little boy on his lap. We asked him if he had time to listen to a message about God and families. He told us that his wife was not home but that "perhaps we could come back the following night."

Of course we could come back! We left with smiles on our faces and gratitude in our hearts. The next night was slow in coming, but finally, the awaited hour arrived. We were greeted with smiles and warmth. We stepped into their clean, two-room, modest wooden home. Their four children under the age of ten, greeted us with the typical shyness, for they were unsure of these strange white-shirted men in their world.

We sat down on two small wooden chairs, while the mom and dad sat on the edge of one chair and the kids on the bed that filled their room. In our broken Spanish, we introduced ourselves and asked them a few questions to get better acquainted with them. We learned that the father recently became unemployed and that the mother was washing peoples' laundry, just to buy rice for their kids.

Our hearts went out to them. They did tell us however, they were confident the father would gain employment soon. After some discussion, we went over the basic steps of how to offer a prayer. They were familiar with praying. We taught them about God, a Heavenly Father, who loves each one of us. We told them about the importance of family unity. We taught them that this life does have a purpose and that we are all special in the eyes of God.

Suddenly, that dim room did not seem so dark after all, as the light of truth replaced the confusion in their minds. Within their eyes, a spark of hope began forming, as the Holy Spirit bore witness to them of our simple testimonies. Their hearts understood what my imperfect words were trying to convey. Their lives were touched, as was mine, as I realized, once again, the importance of this life and the need there is for us to keep trying.

It was several weeks later, that this family confided to me that the night before we visited them, they had prayed to

Heavenly Father to help them find the truth and solace in their lives. My testimony was strengthened and that was the beginning of my ability to understand my purpose here. It was reemphasized, emphatically, when I had the privilege of baptizing the father, mother and three of their children.

Over the months in the mission field, I've come to appreciate and understand my purpose in the Dominican Republic. I have come to see the beauty in the narrow dirt roads. I can now look past the garbage in the streets to see homes, filled with love. I can now see the beauty in dark, shining eyes. The warmth and love I feel from this people takes the chill out of my cold bucket baths. I love my life in this country. I will never be the same person that I left behind, when I came to this country.

Most of all, I have come to realize the change that is brought into lives through a simple belief in God. I am eternally grateful that I have been allowed to be a small part of those changes.

∾

Another valuable lesson I learned on my mission that will make life a little more bearable for me is the gift of laughter. I have concluded that laughter is the most effective way to take the sting out of what may otherwise be terrible. Elbert Hubbard once observed, *"Pain is deeper than all thought; laughter is higher than all pain."* Let me illustrate:

On one particular evening, my missionary companion and I had concluded visiting a family. We mounted our bikes and headed for our apartment. We found ourselves riding in the dark. The electric power had been interrupted in the city, as it often did. We were headed south on Sanchez Boulevard, my companion in front of me, as I pedaled behind him. We were approaching a four-way intersection. As we drew nearer to the intersection, heading north, we noticed a medium-sized pickup truck with its signal light, indicating a left-hand turn. We slowed down, so he could make the turn, but with his arm out the window, he gestured for us to go ahead and pass in front of him.

Big mistake! With my companion still in front of me, we sped up to pass quickly, when suddenly the truck shot forward to make the left hand turn, hitting the back tire of my companion's bike, knocking him to the ground. This all happened very quickly, but I soon saw that my companion was alright. On the other hand, it flashed through my mind that I was not going to get out of that situation without a scratch. In an instant, my front bicycle tire hit the left front wheel of the truck. The impact was so great, that I was thrown over the hood, landing face down on the pavement.

Blood began to pour out of my crushed nose, cracked lips, and cut up chin. Because I was lying on the ground on my right side, the flow of blood seeped down the right side of my white shirt. The next thing I recall, I was being turned over on my back. I could see through my dazed eyes a swarm of people, surrounding me.

Then, suddenly, almost in unison, a group of them, upon noticing my tattered crimson red shirt and no right arm, began screaming, "His arm! His arm! It's gone!"

They all scrambled to search for my lost arm that, perchance, was lying somewhere on the road. Then I heard the next frantic scream, "Ay Dios Mio, it's probably under the truck!" which, by this time had long since sped away, perhaps dropping a finger or thumb at each mile marker.

In the midst of all this confusion, I lay there in pain, trying to convince them to forget about my arm! I had already been missing it for the last fifteen years! It was my nose, my mouth, my chin, my entire face that needed the attention they were frantically paying to a phantom arm!

The wise old Roman, Senecca spoke truly, when he said, *"It is more fitting to laugh at life than to lament over it."* I agree!

CHAPTER 14

Heaven Sent

---

*S*ometimes in life, we are fortunate enough to cross paths with individuals that motivate us to do the impossible, inspire us to conquer our challenges, instill in us a belief that there is a better tomorrow. I have been the recipient of these magnificent qualities, exhibited by people in my life. Yet, some of the more important ingredients, imbedded in my mind and heart are how to live, how to laugh, and how to love.

My beautiful wife, Wendy, my love, my life, my laughter, has given me purpose, direction and perspective throughout our eight years of marriage. How can I describe this queen of my heart, without using cliches; she, who means everything in the world to me? How can I express my feelings about a lady, when there are no words to define her? How can I can share my adoration for a crowning jewel whose love is beyond comparison? There is no other woman, there never was a woman, there will never be another woman, who is the embodiment of my heaven-sent Wendy. I have always said, if there was such a thing as an extension of the eternities, I would request it of God, just so I could spend that much more time at the side of Wendy.

Our story began in 1984. We met at Allied Development Company, a variety store, at 6400 South State Street in Murray, Utah, where we were both employed. I worked in Housewares as a cashier and Wendy Watts was a sales clerk in Sporting Goods. Allied's slogan was, "If we don't have it, you don't need it." Coincidently, they had Wendy and I needed her! However, that dream did not come to fruition for several more years.

At age sixteen, as a new employee at Allied, I can still remember the first time I saw Wendy. I was standing behind my check stand, when Wendy walked in the east doors to begin her shift. As she walked by the check stand, our eyes met. She smiled. I smiled. She continued on to her post. I was completely distracted by her striking beauty. I couldn't take my eyes off of her, as she made her way to her department. Her stunning, radiant smile penetrated my heart like a sharp sword. She left me breathless with her almond-shaded, roguish eyes. Her light brown hair fell softly on her shoulders as she sauntered, confidently, through the aisles.

I had to meet her!

So, I made it a point that whenever items that belonged to sporting goods needed to be returned, I was the one to do it, just so I could have a chance to talk with her. We became a bit more acquainted with one another, when we occasionally went out, as a group, with several other employees. For reasons not clear to me now, I didn't pursue Wendy, romantically, during the time we did things with our other friends. Wendy was then involved with a boyfriend. I became serious with another girl. And so, it seemed we were destined to be only good friends.

During the summer of 1985, I departed for my mission to the Dominican Republic. Wendy remained employed at Allied, and corresponded with me through mail—a lot at first, and then a letter, here and there.

Meanwhile, Wendy went on to graduate from Jordan High School and moved to Montville, New Jersey in 1986 to work as a nanny and to attend a business college. After I returned from my mission, I rekindled my relationship with my girlfriend. However, after several months, she decided she wanted to go on a mission herself. And so, she went.

Sometime in March 1988, while browsing through my trusty address book, I came across Wendy's name. I dialed the number. Her mother told me Wendy was still living in New Jersey. I got her number and called. She was pleasantly surprised to hear from me. It so happened that, just a week before receiving my phone call, Wendy had decided she was going to come home to Utah. We arranged that when she arrived home, she would contact me and we would get together and renew acquaintances.

Some time in April, 1988, after being home a few weeks, Wendy telephoned me and agreed to meet me at my work. I found her still as beautiful as ever! We started going out together, every Tuesday, just as friends, getting together to pass the time. As the weeks passed, our relationship progressed, and deeper emotions emerged. By late fall of 1988 Wendy and I grew increasingly closer, until we came to realize that we had fallen in love and wanted to share our lives together.

On December 23, 1988, I asked Wendy to marry me. It was after my family's Christmas party. I picked Wendy up at her catering job, working in a residential home. She was dressed in her formal attire. I drove her in a car through the Capitol Heights neighborhood, just west of the University of Utah, until we reached the location where I was going to ask her "THE QUESTION."

She had an inquisitive look on her face, puzzled as to what we were doing in this area. We got out of the car, and I escorted Wendy (in a dress and tennis shoes) through nearly a foot of freshly-fallen snow to the large, concrete letter "U" that dominates the hills above the neighborhood. The "U" (outlined with light bulbs) is an emblem for the University of Utah. Coincidently, the university basketball team had won their game that evening. To signal their win, the "U" flashed on and off, throughout the evening.

We stood in the midst of the brilliance of this concrete slab, overlooking downtown Salt Lake City, embraced in each other's arms. We were reminded of the cool and crisp air with every breath we took. A slight breeze calmly rippled through our hair, as if to whisper in our ears that tonight was a perfect night to dedicate our lives to each other. I then directed her eyes to the State Capitol Building and asked her if she could see it. She nodded, yes. Next, I focused her attention on the LDS Church office building, adjacent to it.

Then, pointing to the magnificent structure of the Salt Lake Temple, I said, "Can you see the Salt Lake Temple?" "Yes!" she responded. Anxiously I said, "Wendy, will you marry me in that temple?" Before she answered me she blubbered, "Where's my ring?" From out of my coat pocket I pulled the ring box, and while I, nervously, opened it, she cried out an enthusiastic "Yes!"

We chose May 5, 1989 as our wedding day. We couldn't have asked for a better day to get married. The weather cooperated nicely, with a perfect eighty degrees. The ceremony, wedding breakfast and reception went without a hitch. I can remember feeling extremely overjoyed, throughout the day.

Nothing could have spoiled that special day in our lives.

From that day forward, we vowed to be faithful, committed, and devoted to one another. We promised we would stick together through the good times and the bad times, encourage each other through the ups and downs, and strengthen one another through both sorrowful and happy moments. We regard our marriage as sacred, and wholly reserved for those who respect the vows of matrimony.

Marriage should not be considered as just another phase in our lives. Rather, It should be honored as a wholesome covenant between husband and wife, as a means to achieve oneness in purpose. If we adhere to this level of sanctity, we will choose more carefully the words we use, so as not to demean or belittle our spouse. We will learn to control our tempers, so that we need not be sorry for our actions. We will discipline ourselves to change our behavior, so as not to be offensive. We will care, not criticize. We will revere, not rebuke. We will protect, not punish. We will love, not lust.

It is the simple, yet indisputable truth: We can all improve our marriages. Wendy and I work hard at our relationship. Every day becomes easier; every year becomes better. I love Wendy more today, than the day I asked her to marry me. In fact, I can't wait until tomorrow, because I will love her even more!

CHAPTER 15

Fatherhood

---

*W*endy and I always knew that having children would add a new dimension to our marriage. However, we never expected it to be so rewarding. Today we bask in the joys of parenthood. We are proud parents of three beautiful and wonderful children.

Our oldest boy, Johvan Padilla Davis, was born August 16, 1991, a healthy 8 pounds 3 ounces, with lots of dark hair. I can still remember the day of his birth. Several hours after he was born, I left Wendy and Johvan to themselves in the delivery room. I walked to an empty room where I could be alone. I was so overcome with joy, witnessing the birth of my son, I needed to kneel down and pray to thank the Lord for the new little miracle that had just blessed our lives. Being inexperienced in this new calling of fatherhood, I asked the Lord to give me the strength and the fortitude necessary to carry out my responsibilities as a parent. I realized then and there, that 99.9 percent of Wendy's and my time and effort would be directed to our children, until they depart from home.

For the first five months of his life, I was Mr. Mom to Johvan while Wendy worked part-time. I changed his diapers, bathed him, dressed him, and fed him. I did everything for him. As stressful as I found it to be sometimes, I was fortunate enough to have spent those precious months caring for him. Some of my favorite moments were when I held him in my arm, snuggled up close to me. I rocked him to sleep while singing, "You are so beautiful." There was an angelic look to him as he calmly dozed off to sleep.

Today, as a seven-year-old, Johvan, is a well-mannered, well-behaved child. He is extremely helpful to his mother with chores around the home, sharing with his younger sister, and babysitting his baby brother. His school teacher praises him effusively about his good behavior in class. We hope and pray these positive traits continue with him through the remainder of his school years. Wendy and I can never say often enough, what a heaven-sent child he has been to us.

To give you an idea of his tender nature, while driving home one evening from running errands, I noticed from the rear view mirror, Johvan intensely staring up to the star-filled, moonlit sky. Inquisitively, I turned to Johvan to ask him what he was thinking about. While maintaining his gaze out the window, he responded with a soft voice, "Dad, do you know what I am going to do for you?"

"What, son?"

"I'm going to climb a ladder and pull down the moon so you can play with it."

"I would like that, Johvan." Johvan would give you the world if he could.

Wendy and I wanted a little girl so we could name her after Luz. Almost three and a half years after Johvan was born, our home was blessed with another little spirit. Elysha Luz Davis was born July 8, 1994, a healthy 7 pounds 5 ounces. From the beginning, she had a sparkle to her big brown eyes and a glow to her countenance. Her delicate facial features remind me of a beautifully sculptured porcelain doll. Her radiant smile compliments her glowing personality.

I think, as a parent, I am entitled to wax poetic about gorgeous children. Ely, as we call her, is an absolute doll! We will be stopped in malls, stores, and restaurants by people, just so they can have a closer look at our kids, especially Ely. They compliment us and her on how strikingly beautiful she is. Sometimes, we think, what have we started here? All this attention hasn't gone to her three-year-old head, yet. We hope it never does. But for now, I like the fact that the two most stunningly gorgeous women in the entire world live in my home!

Besides having a pretty face, Ely, is very intelligent. I am constantly impressed how well she communicates and expresses herself with her limited vocabulary and pronunciation. She counts to fifteen, but in the interim, she created her own number, "eleventeen." She has mastered the alphabet all the way to, "next time won't you sing with me." Even though she can't read yet, she will memorize stories read to her and will pretend reading to her younger brother.

Ely also has the ability to make people laugh. She will do quirky and silly things that will make you chuckle. Like putting on Johvan's clothes, three times her size, from head to toe, and walking around the house, pretending to be him. Or she will mimic things she has heard Wendy and I say to Johvan in her own demanding little voice: "Johvan, clean your room, or I'll put you in time out!" Ely makes me laugh!

Ely does have a reverent side to her, as well. She loves to

offer prayer at the dinner table, even when one has been offered, already. She enjoys listening to scripture stories at our church's nursery and at home.

I treasure the moments, whenever I hear her sweet small voice say, "I love you dada!"

Our youngest son, Raeben Brett Davis, was born October 15, 1996 at 6 pounds 7 ounces. His precious little spirit has already illuminated our home with joy and happiness. He truly is a special boy!

Wendy and I often comment on the glimmering aura Raeben radiates through his precious little countenance. It is as if we have been placed in charge of a heavenly angel. There is something about him that tells us he is not just another ordinary boy. He has been given the official title of "sweet boy."

At eighteen months old, big brown eyes and with a full set of teeth, Raeben, walks, talks, falls, runs, laughs, cries and exhausts mom and dad. He is constantly busy getting into things. Pulling toys out from the toy-box, taking clothes out from the kids dressers, making a mess of the kitchen with pots and pans and utensils and unrolling toilet tissue all over the bathroom. Well, you get the idea of his daily activities. There is never a dull moment with Raeben around.

It is so exciting to watch him develop right before our very eyes! Every day, he accomplishes new things. Before we know it, he will be grown and out of the home. But as long as he is with us, I will savor my time with him. Besides, he will always be my "sweet boy."

I can't help but blubber about my children. I could go on and on about them. I love being a father. With it comes a lot of responsibility. I like to think I have been trained along the way for this great calling by my natural parents, Luz, Tia Mary, doctors, nurses, Mom and Dad, Wendy and others. I feel confident that what I have learned from them I can instill in my children.

Johvan   Wendy   Raeben   Abel   Elysha
Padilla   Brett   Luz

CHAPTER 16

Walking on a Tightrope

In my profession as a motivational speaker, I have the occasion to travel to various places and converse with people from all walks of life. I am encouraged by the efforts individuals are expending to make significant improvements in their lives for the better. But it is also an eye opening experience to witness the sorrow, the anguish, the hurt, the bitterness, and the suffering with which people burden themselves. I am bewildered at how many people believe there is no hope, no chance, no avenue, no opportunity, no way to purge themselves of their self-imposed misery, poverty and self-doubt. I believe each individual has the personal capacity to master their conditions of obscurity by simply energizing the pertinent principles that one innately possesses. I would like to illustrate how one can eradicate self-defeating behavioral patterns by living a life as a "Tightrope Walker."

I was eleven years old when my Mom and Dad took me and my younger brothers and sisters to see the Shrine Circus that had just come into town at the old Salt Palace Arena in downtown Salt Lake City. As I sat in my seat, waiting with anticipation to witness my very first circus show, the lights dimmed and a spotlight focused on the Ring Master. Then, through the loud speakers, his voice echoed enthusiastically "Ladies and gentlemen! Boys and girls! Welcome to the Greatest Show on Earth!"

The whole evening was captivating for me to watch the different events of the circus. I was amused by the enormous performing elephants, who could stand on their front legs, walk on their hind feet, and perform balancing acts on balls. I was clearly fascinated by the lion tamer, who boldly placed his entire head into the open mouth of a ferocious lion. Not a very smart guy if you ask me! I was intrigued by the human cannonball who was shot out of a makeshift cannon, flying through the air and landing safely in a net at the other end of the arena.

I was mesmerized by the trapeze artists who would courageously do all kinds of flips and stunts in mid-air, high above ground, placing unbounded confidence in their partners to catch them in mid-flight. A circus would not be a circus without the hilarious clowns. With painted faces and goofy gags, they went to great lengths to get the audience to laugh.

Of all the events mentioned, one in particular left a powerful impression on my mind: the Tightrope Walker. I will elaborate further on that performer, and point out the parallels in our own lives. For there are many lessons I have learned from the difficult, yet ultimately simple act of walking a tight rope.

I don't claim to be an expert on the profession of tightrope walking, but I believe that it is safe to assume it commands numerous hours of training and countless hours of practice. That was evident, as I watched the tightrope walker standing on the small platform high above ground, prepared to take his initial steps on the long, thin rope. His main goal was to reach the other side without incident. That required intense focus and total concentration.

The walker waved his arm to the Ring Master to start the drum roll. But, before he took his first steps, he grasped a long pole to give him balance and to aid his equilibrium. He was cautious with each step, careful with each move. At one point, I noticed he was about to lose his balance and looked as though he was going to fall. My heart began beating faster at the notion he might be plunging to the ground, one hundred feet below him. His well-orchestrated performance created excitement in the crowd. Palpably, the crowd wanted him to fail and fall off the rope. To my surprise, the walker did fall! Even though I had wanted him to fall, I gasped a sigh of relief when he landed safely in the safety net. To prove to the audience that he could really cross the rope, he immediately sprang from the net, climbed back up the ladder and proceeded to undertake the effort, all over again. Undaunted, he re-traced his steps and was successful on the second attempt. Once he reached the other side the crowd cheered and applauded his accomplishment.

It takes discipline, courage, patience and perseverence to be a tightrope walker. It takes similar traits and habits to walk, successfully, through the journey of life. We must not lose sight of how fragile and narrow the road is ahead of us. Just as the tightrope walker depended on a pole to provide balance to his steps, we also need to rely on our God-given gifts and the service of others to give us stability and direction as we journey through the course of our existence. Our goal in life should be joy and contentment which are only achieved by steady performance, controlled behavior, and a focused attitude.

However, discontentment, failures, obstacles, and sorrow lie in wait in curves, gutters, forks, bends and intersections.

More often than not, I have surrendered myself to such feelings of hopelessness, and fallen victim to some of these deceptions. My pain has been great. My sorrow has been deep. The important lesson to learn here is: there must be opposition in all things. You cannot have success without failure. You cannot experience happiness without sadness. You cannot have joy without sorrow.

Therefore, I have come to appreciate that every sorrow can be vanquished, every failure can be defeated, every obstacle can be conquered. However, in the event we detour from our course and experience suffering, we also have our safety net to fall on: perseverance and encouragement from others. If we have been beaten up, trodden down or fallen off, we need not give up; these are only temporary setbacks. Muster up the courage and summon the strength that is essential to get back on board to continue your quest.

It is also interesting to note that we are quick to judge other people's short-comings. I believe we do it, because, (1) we are ignorant, insensitive slobs, and/or (2) it brings them down to our own diminutive level. Misery loves company! It is detrimental to our own progression, if we think we are doing a service by putting people down. Let us not scoff, mock, scorn and ridicule another's short-comings. Luring people to destruction only brings misery and disappointment. This kind of conduct reminds me of when I wanted to see the tightrope walker fall off the rope and fail in his goal to reach the other side, just to satisfy my craving for excitement. Instead, let us stretch forth our hearts and lend a helping hand by encouraging, sustaining and supporting others to achieve their goals and accomplish their dreams.

Let us leave no one "out on a limb!"

Finally, my thoughts reflect on the gratifying feeling and a sense of accomplishment the tightrope walker must have finally felt to reach the other side of the rope, after a lot of hard work. Every day we are challenged at work, school, home, and at play to be our personal best. Every day we make decisions and choices that determine our moral character. No matter who we are, to reach the pinnacle of success, we must climb the highest mountain, sail the widest ocean, and swim the longest river. Doing so, builds confidence, determination, and self-worth. Ponder how pleased we will be with ourselves, to have crossed the finish line and persevered to the end. How gratified we will be in knowing that we did everything possible to make life worth it! How blessed we will be, one day, to hear a sweet voice say, "Well done my good and faithful servant."

Since the publication of this book, several new exciting developments have transpired. After 28 years, I've made contact with my birth mother. I am informed I have six unknown siblings and that they are doing well. This remarkable discovery has embedded in my heart a yearning to surround myself with their longing love. I envision a wonderful reunion filled with joy, laughter and tears. This new chapter in my life will have a positive impact on my family and add a new dimension to my already extraordinary life.

To make this journey complete, I will be traveling to Bolivia in September 1998 to unite with my family and relish in their warm embrace and love.

To be continued. . . .

The One-Armed Wordsmith

In Admiration for Abel Davis

He often said he loved to work with words,
As other craftsmen crave to shape the wood.
He sent his syllables, like blessed birds,
To make his missives better understood.
He gripped the alphabet, like shards of oak,
And carved it into rhymes. He often spoke
In parables and metaphors to gain
The luminescent longings of his soul

Like rare mahogany with ruddy grain,
His polished words became a sacred scroll.
The nouns and verbs he used as building blocks,
To fitly frame the sentences he carved.
His regal rhyming schemes, unorthodox,
Transcended reason, even when he starved.
The dictionary was his trusted friend
To store his wondrous words until the end.

Each letter, shining with intrinsic worth,
Spelled out the precious tools with which he wrote.
And, like a pregnant poet, giving birth,
He fashioned his poetic anecdote.
He loved alliteration in his rhymes.
Without his arm, he wrote and wondered why
The lessons of the language of his times,
Would often wall within and make him cry.

He loved to see his adjectives infused
In modifying every noun he used.
Like venting varnish on some thirsty wood,
He brushed his perfect adjectives upon
The nervous nouns, as naked as they stood
(How well, he once described a mastodon!)
Simplicity, for him, became the key
In weaving words into an ode or sonnet.

His heart had hungered in that mystery,
In searching where and how to latch upon it.
For only syllables that touch the soul
Create a crystal from a lump of coal.
Who knows the alchemy his words impart
To someone seeking light? The wordsmith shows
The power he commands to heal the heart.
His single hand writes what he truly knows.

The blacksmith and the silversmith are known
For skills in working metals all their lives.
With torch and tools they often stand alone
In making sure their industry survives.
But he who fashions words that often rhyme,
Reflects the gentle people of his time.
The great events and monuments, he tells;
Celebrities and Congress, he reports.

He covers county fairs and wishing wells.
He even writes, poetically, of sports.
But, most of all, the people he proclaims:
The ordinary folks with modest means.
They, usually, have ordinary names,
While following conventional routines.
He scans his brain to find the perfect world,
So what he writes will never sound absurd.

He knows more-abled men may shape the wood;
His craft is used to make things understood.
His rhymes are written, much like people speak;
Like polished wood; authentic and unique!
The one-armed wordsmith works a special skill
To ply his craft with jet-black ink and quill.
He is a very independent chap:
Whoever said he had a handicap?

— Clyde E. Weeks, Jr.